José Luis Illanes

# On the
# Theology
# of Work

# José Luis Illanes

# On the Theology of Work

## Aspects of the teaching of the founder of Opus Dei

FOUR COURTS PRESS / SCEPTER

This book, typeset and printed in the Republic of Ireland, is a translation made by Michael Adams of *La santificación del trabajo*, sixth edition, Madrid 1980.

© original, Ediciones Palabra, S.A., Alcalá 55, Madrid-14 1980

© translation, Four Courts Press Limited, Kill Lane, Blackrock, Co. Dublin, Ireland 1982

ISBN 0 906127 55 6  cloth bound edition
ISBN 0 906127 56 4  paperbound edition

Published in North America by Scepter Press, 481 Main Street, Suite 401, New Rochelle, N.Y. 10801.

 British Library Cataloguing in Publication Data


Illanes, José Luis
On the theology of work.
1. Opus Dei
I. Title
267'.182      BX809.S49

ISBN 0-906127-55-6
ISBN 0-906127-56-4  Pbk

# CONTENTS

91430

# PREFACE

On 26 June 1975 Monsignor Josemaría Escrivá de Balaguer, the founder of Opus Dei, died in Rome. The news media at the time highlighted his reputation for holiness, the importance of his life and the fruitful furrow he had opened up in the history of the Church. Some months later, in September of the same year, members of Opus Dei from all over the world met in Rome and unanimously elected the founder's closest aide, Alvaro del Portillo y Diez de Sollano, as his successor as President General. Immediately afterwards, addressing the press, Fr Alvaro del Portillo spoke of how the spirit of Opus Dei showed 'people how to immerse themselves in all noble human activities, to involve themselves in a Christian way, in God's presence, in all those things of the earth which men and women love in a pure and upright way'. He stressed that 'family life, daily work, the rights and duties that life in society implies, in other words everything which goes to make up a person's ordinary life, can be sanctified'.[1]

In June 1976, in an article to mark the first anniversary of Monsignor Escrivá's death, he again referred to the universal call to holiness, to the sanctification of work, to viewing marriage as a Christian vocation. . . . Monsignor Escrivá, through his contribution in all these fields, was, he said, 'one of the great precursors of the second Vatican Council'.[2]

Very many Churchmen have spoken or written along similar lines. One of these testimonies calls for special mention: Pope John Paul II, in a homily on 19 August 1979 addressed to a group of members of Opus Dei, said, 'Your institution has as its aim the sanctification of ordinary life while remaining in the world, in your own work setting: living the Gospel in the world, living completely immersed in the world but with the purpose of transforming it and redeeming it through your own love for Christ. Yours is truly a great ideal – an ideal which from its very beginning anticipated that theology of the laity which later characterised the Church of the Council and of the post-conciliar period.'[3]

One year before, on 25 July 1978, Cardinal Albino Luciani, very soon afterwards to become John Paul I, published an article on 'Seeking God through everyday work' in which he touched on certain aspects of the spirituality of Opus Dei. He showed its historic importance by comparing Monsignor Escrivá with one of the great modern saints, Francis de Sales, famous for his pastoral concern for ordinary Christians who devote themselves to secular activities: 'Monsignor Escrivá', he wrote, 'went further than Francis de Sales in many respects. Saint Francis proclaimed sanctity for everyone but seems to have taught only a "spirituality for lay people" whereas Monsignor Escrivá wants a "lay spirituality". Francis, in other words, nearly always suggests the same practical means as used by religious, but with suitable modifications. Escrivá is more radical: he goes as far as talking about "materialising" – in a good sense – the quest for holiness. For him it is the very material work itself that must be turned into prayer and holiness'[4].

Another quotation of this sort is from Cardinal Sebastiano Baggio, the prefect of the Sacred Congregation for Bishops and someone who had known Monsignor Escrivá since he first went to live in Rome in 1946: 'It is evident even today that the life, work and message of Monsignor Escrivá de Balaguer constitute a new departure or, better, a new chapter in the history of Christian spirituality. Throughout the history of the Church, he comments, there have been many preachers and directors of souls who have invited everyone, whatever his or her situation in life, to follow Christ's way really seriously; but, he adds, 'what continues to be revolutionary in the spiritual message of Monsignor Escrivá de Balaguer is his practical manner of directing men and women of every condition in life to Christian holiness. This practical realisation of his message is based on three new aspects which are characteristic of the spirituality of Opus Dei: (1) the Christian laity should not abandon nor despise the world, but should remain within it, loving and sharing the life of ordinary men and women; (2) while staying in the world, they should learn to discover the supernatural value of the normal circumstances of their lives, including the most prosaic and material details; (3) as a consequence, everyday work, the activity which occupies and fills the greatest number of hours of ordinary people, can and should be sanctified and used as a means of Christian apostolate'.[5]

In the early part of 1965 I worked on an essay which was published soon afterwards in *Studi Cattolici* (Milan). The Vatican Council was in full swing: it had just issued its dogmatic constitution *Lumen gentium* in which it had proclaimed, solemnly, the universal call to holiness, the full share that lay people have in the Church's mission, the Christian value of temporal or earthly realities. I tried in that essay to show the coincidence of this teaching of the Magisterium with the spirit which had animated Opus Dei since its foundation in 1928. I also wanted to indicate the significance of Opus Dei in the history of Christian spirituality, precisely because of its contribution to the evaluation of an absolutely essential aspect of our earthly existence, the phenomenon of work and particularly of what I called 'professional work', meaning not the work of people of the 'professional class' but professional work in the sense of work undertaken as a stable condition of one's life, work by which one is involved in everyday society, i.e. not just work as 'occupation of time'. Revising the text two years later (published in English under the title *On the theology of work*: Dublin 1967) I referred to other, later, Council documents which contained important references to work: the decree *Apostolicam actuositatem* (nos. 2-4 and 6-8) and the pastoral constitution *Gaudium et spes* (nos. 22, 33-39, 43, 57, 67). However, I referred to them only incidentally, without reworking the text, because that was unnecessary at the time. Since then things have changed, not only in the sense that we can now see the subject in better perspective but particularly because I now have many new sources to draw on which show the teaching of the founder of Opus Dei.

For the first version of this essay I relied mainly on Monsignor Escrivá de Balaguer's best known book *The Way\** and on some other texts deriving from his catechesis and teaching, notes taken from things he said, which I was able to consult. Soon afterwards, in 1966-68, Monsignor Escrivá gave a series of interviews to European and American journalists which were later collected in a book called *Conversations with Monsignor Escrivá de Balaguer* (first edition 1968).\*\* After that he began to prepare for publication some of the very many homilies he had preached throughout years of intense pastoral work; to date some 39 homilies have been published, ranging in origin from 1941 to 1973, and most of them collected in two books *Christ is passing by* (first edition 1973)‡ and *Friends of God* (first edition 1977).‡

This fund of new material stirred me to tackle once more the job I had first undertaken fourteen years earlier. To have done so in a really thorough way, using all the ideas and nuances in these sources, would have meant setting aside my original essay and starting a completely

---

\*   Current edition Dublin 1981; referred to in the text of this book as Way followed by point number: thus: (Way 440).

\*\*   Current edition Dublin 1980: referred to in the text of this book with its marginal, not page, number: thus: (Conversations 117).

‡   Forthcoming edition Dublin 1982; referred to in the text of this book with its marginal number: thus: (Christ passing 183).

‡   Current edition Dublin 1981; referred to in the text of this book with its marginal number: thus: (Friends 47).

new book. I thought of doing just that; but I have in fact gone in a different direction, for my original essay is still perfectly valid. What I have done is fill it out, but keeping the general structure and focus of the first essay. This does mean that the founder's published texts contain a wealth of material which I have not used, but I am sure that others will explore them later. This approach has also given me the satisfaction of finishing this new version in 1979, in between the fiftieth anniversary of two foundation dates of Opus Dei – 2 October 1978, when the Work first saw the light of day, and 14 February 1930, when it was completed by the foundation of its Women's Branch.

Pamplona, 8 December 1979
Feast of the Immaculate Conception

# I  INTRODUCTION:

## SPIRITUAL THEOLOGY REDISCOVERS
## THE SUBJECT OF WORK

'Their secular character is proper and specific to the laity. . . . By reason of their special vocation it belongs to the laity to seek the kingdom of God by engaging in temporal affairs and directing them according to God's will. They live in the world, that is, they are engaged in each and every work and business of the earth and in the ordinary circumstances of social and family life, which, as it were, constitute their very existence'. Vatican II's constitution *Lumen gentium* uses these words to outline the distinctive characteristics of the laity as an integral part of the people of God.[6]

The purely negative definition of the laity as those who are neither clerics nor religious has thus given way to a positive description which stresses both their belonging to the people of God, being incorporated into Christ, and the fact that they carry out a mission in the world, right in the middle of temporal structures.[7]

The same theological insight is to be found in the next chapter, on the calling of all men to holiness: ' . . . all Christians, whatever may be their state or rank in life, are called to the fullness of the Christian life and to the fulfilment of love. . . . All Christians in the various conditions, tasks and circumstances of their lives and through all these things will be brought to an ever greater holiness if they receive all in faith from the hand of the heavenly Father, and give their co-operation to the divine will, showing forth to all men in temporal service itself the charity with which God has loved the world'. What is particularly interesting here is that *Lumen gentium* states not only that one may aspire to holiness from any state in life but that one should look for holiness precisely by means of that state. Just before this, when referring to manual work, the Council Fathers had written: 'those whose lives are spent in labour ... should make use of human work to fulfil themselves'.[8]

There is a clear connection between both chapters: if lay people are

11

called by God to live in the middle of temporal structures, it is there that they should find the means of holiness. Work, that is, man's job, is , presented as something that is deeply inserted into the supernatural sphere.[9]

This treatment of work in *Lumen gentium* is developed in other conciliar and papal documents to give the central elements for a study of its sanctifying value:

(a) for one thing, the Council brings together and comments on the basic Christian reasons for the dignity of work. Perhaps the most graphic example is the following passage from *Gaudium et spes* 34: 'Individual and collective activity, that monumental effort of man through the centuries to improve the circumstances of the world, presents no problem to believers: considered in itself, it corresponds to the plan of God . . . All this holds good also for our daily work. When men and women provide for themselves and their families in such a way as to be of service to the community as well, they can rightly look upon their work as a prolongation of the work of the Creator, a service to their fellow men, and their personal contribution to the fulfilment in history of the divine plan'. The same teaching is to be found in Pope Paul VI's encyclical *Populorum progressio*: 'God, who has endowed man with intelligence, imagination and sensitivity, has also given him the means of, somehow completing his work.'[10] Human activity, work, is part of the order of things willed by God – and this is not a static order; it reflects God's perfection in a dynamic way. Creation is not only something that has happened: it is happening.[11]

(b) Parallel to this dogmatic and cosmic perspective there is a more directly anthropological consideration which shows the contribution of work to man's own perfection, supernatural as well as human. The decree on the apostolate of the laity develops this idea when outlining the general features of the spiritual life of lay people: 'Laymen should make such a use of these helps [various spiritual exercises and the liturgy] that, while meeting their human obligations in the ordinary conditions of life, they do not separate their union with Christ from their ordinary life: but through the very performance of their tasks, which are God's will for them, actually promote the growth of their union with him. . . . This lay spirituality will take its particular character from the circumstances of one's state in life (married and family life, celibacy, widowhood), from one's state of health and from one's professional and social activity. Whatever the circumstances, each one has received suitable talents and these should be cultivated as should also the personal gifts he has from the Holy Spirit.'[12]

As Paul VI put it, 'Not only must a man convert his profession into something good, not only must he sanctify it, but the profession itself must be looked upon as something that perfects and leads to holiness. It is not necessary to leave one's way to be worthy of the Gospel and of Christ. It is enough to stay where one is, to remain there, giving one's own duties that attention and loyalty which turn a man into a person who is good, honest, just and exemplary'.[13]

The doctrinal reach and historic importance of these statements becomes clearer when you realise that even a few years earlier this sort of language would have been inconceivable. In other words, spiritual theology knew nothing, said nothing, about the subject of work. If you look at three of the best known manuals of spiritual theology you find, for example, in Tanqueray (first published in 1923) only three pages devoted to the sanctification of work, and even this comes under the heading of 'Sanctification of social relations'. In *The Three Ages of the Interior Life* by Garrigou-Lagrange (1938) and *Theologia Spiritualis* by de Guibert of the Gregorian University (1937) there is no mention whatever of work or indeed of the duties of one's state in life.

What is the reason for this? Although I shall go into it in more detail later on, I can outline here the background to it. It is connected partly with the influence of monastic theology on spiritual theology. Of course, it must be said first of all that all the spiritualities which have flourished in the Church over the centuries are to be valued for their faithfulness to the Gospel, which Church approval guarantees. Any gaps or shortcomings are imputable, rather, to later theological reflection which sometimes did sin by imbalance, by not trying to get a total overview of its subject. This particular spiritual theology tended to look at Christian spirituality in general through the prism of being cut off from the world, and failed to see it also from the viewpoint of the person rooted in that world: it forgot, or in practice neglected, to pay attention to the values proper to the lay person's experience of life.[14]

Another relevant factor is the rupture which, deriving from a complex historical process, was created from the middle of the eighteenth century onwards, between the secular world and the ecclesiastical world, between philosophy and theology — a rupture which was reinforced by deistic and atheistic ideologies. Religion was brushed aside: it was of no importance; it was even something dangerous. It would have been bad enough if this tendency resulted in separating work life from Christian life, but it went farther than that: it actually argued that the two were in opposition to one another. Paul VI put it this way, when he was still Cardinal Montini: 'Religion and work. Today these two expressions of human life are not only distinct but separate: they ignore, suspect or actually oppose one another. Often they live side by side but do not help each other or fuse in a homogeneous spirituality or meet in a balanced harmony. When forced to come close they do so fearfully: religion puts obstacles in the other's path and work insults religion. One would think that they were made not to go together, that the worker's opposition to religion is deep and insoluble.'[15]

Five years later, when he had become pope, during the Vatican Council, he spoke often about this problem, showing his deep, apostolic concern. As he put it to a congress of young workers: 'It is up to you to bring Christ, to bring him again, into the world of work, and especially into the new generations of workers. It is not a matter of making extremist propaganda or becoming pietistic, much less of forming closed groups or feeling aloof from the worker's life. It is not a matter of depriving this life of work of its spiritual dignity, of its religious and moral values; rather, it means infusing into work a Christian and human meaning which ennobles, strengthens, purifies, comforts and fills it with good sentiments of solidarity and friendship, and helps one to defend one's economic and professional interests in a spirit of justice and understanding for the common good. Does not your faith, your Christian conscience, your religious conviction give you the most exalted, sure and happy sense of life? That is what faith is for: to be useful for life.'[16]

We shall always have to strive for this synthesis of religion and work that the Pope urges in his addresses. It does not just happen. It will always be up to our freedom to achieve it. But it is already something to make Christians *aware* of the problem; the Vatican II texts I have already quoted do this, in their attempt to have the Church 'arrive at fuller definition of herself.'[17] So we can speak of there being a new theological situation, a rediscovery by spiritual theology of the subject of work. There has been definite progress. The rediscovery of work is one of those steps forward by which the Church, gathering up her past, integrates it in a desire for greater fidelity to Christ and to the word he has handed down to us. It is an event which shows forth the living presence of the Spirit. Monsignor Escrivá, writing in 1948, put it this way: 'The Church, which is a living body, shows her vitality through the interior movement which gives her life. This movement is often something more than a mere adaptation to environment: it is a vigorous and confident injection into that environment. The Church, led by the Holy Spirit, does not pass through this world as in an obstacle race, trying to avoid the obstacles; nor does she follow the broad meanderings of life, along the line of least resistance; on the contrary,

14

she walks on earth with a firm and sure step; she opens up a way.'[18]

Earlier I asked why it was that spiritual theology had forgotten all about work. Now I might ask: what specifically led to its rediscovery of work; what factors have contributed to this new insight into the sanctifying value of work?

'It is the Holy Spirit who provides the new people of God with its spirituality,'[19] writes Michael Schmaus in his treatise on the Church. It is He who enlivens and increases the Body of Christ. Great changes and movements in the Church are not the result of natural forces or even of human meditation on the word of God: it is the Holy Spirit who weaves a pattern towards that measure of the fullness of Christ at which the Church aims (cf Eph 4:13). It is not possible to explain the history of the Church by theorising alone; this history must be examined with the eyes of faith. Newman has shown the importance of practice, experience and life in the evolution and development of Catholic doctrine.[20] And if his thesis holds true for all areas of doctrine, it is especially true of spiritual theology.

Of course, many other factors play their part. For example there are the cultural and social movements, Christian in inspiration, which arose in response to the problems posed by the industrial revolution and the dechristianization of large sectors of society; these led, though sometimes indirectly, to a study of the role of the spiritual life as the basis of action.[21] I should also refer to theological studies, sometimes provoked by the pastoral needs of the Church, sometimes deriving from the development of biblical and patristic studies.[22] And particularly I should mention those spiritual movements, the fruit of that very action of the Holy Spirit who breathes where and as he wishes (cf Jn 3:8), calling Christians to greater fidelity to Christ, to greater docility to his word.

In the history of these spiritual movements one event has special relevance – the birth of Opus Dei in 1928 and its subsequent development. I would say in fact that the spirit and activity of Opus Dei have been one of the ways chosen by the Holy Spirit to provoke the current renewal and lead to a deepening awareness of the supernatural value of work.[23]

In this essay I want to examine some of the main features of Opus Dei's spirituality, examining it in itself and in relation to the whole range of Christian spirituality over the centuries.[24]

# II OPUS DEI AND THE EVALUATION OF WORK:

## NOTES FOR A HISTORY OF SPIRITUALITY

*Re-reading Scripture*

'Opus Dei, both in the training it gives its members and in the way it goes about its apostolates, is based on each member sanctifying his daily work': these words come from an address by Monsignor Escrivá on 21 November 1965 in the presence of Paul VI and a group of bishops and cardinals; the occasion was the opening of the Centro ELIS, a technical training centre for young workers which the Holy See had asked members of Opus Dei to run.[25] Some months later he said to a French journalist: 'Ever since 1928 I have been preaching that sanctity is not reserved for the privileged few and that all the ways of the earth can be divine. The reason is that the spirituality of Opus Dei is based on the sanctification of ordinary work' (Conversations 34).[26]

The founder of Opus Dei was constantly speaking along those lines. 'We have come to say', he said on 24 March 1930, 'with the humility of someone who knows he is a sinner and of no importance – *homo peccator sum* (Lk 5:8), we can say with Peter – but with the faith of someone who allows himself to be guided by God's hand: we have come to say that holiness is not something for the privileged few: God calls everyone, Love awaits all of us: everyone, no matter where he may be; everyone, no matter what his state in life, his profession or trade. For that ordinary everyday life, apparently unimportant, can be a means to holiness.'*

Where did Monsignor Escrivá get this certainty, this deep conviction that work could be hallowed and that it could be a way to holiness? He got it from a divine insight, on 2 October 1928, which showed him he should devote his whole life to getting people in all walks of life to look for holiness in the middle of the world, in the fulfilment of their every-

---

* In future when quoting as yet unpublished material taken from Monsignor Escrivá's catechesis I shall tend simply to give the date of the text in the body of my essay, in parentheses, after the quotation.

day work.[27] From that moment onwards he was forever proclaiming in one way or another the Christian meaning of work.

In proclaiming this teaching he made vivid use of texts from sacred Scripture. 'Old as the Gospel and like the Gospel new' was how he described the message of Opus Dei. Reading the Bible in the light of that inspiration which he first got in 1928 he was able to discover a new wealth of meaning; a whole series of passages in the Old and New Testaments took on a new importance.

'Convinced that man has been created *ut operaretur* (Gen 2:15), we know well that ordinary work is the hinge of our holiness and the right supernatural and human means of bearing Christ with us and allowing us to do good to all' (14 February 1950). This commandment to work, given by God at the very beginning of history, was a favourite reference point of the founder of Opus Dei in his preaching: God created man to work; that was his intention, even before man sinned: work is not a curse or punishment; no: work is a way, an opportunity, to share in God's plans.[28]

The Christian needs to assimilate this truth: he needs to have a positive view of work, to discover in the commandment to work a law which, because it is divine, raises man up and ennobles him. 'After many centuries we have reminded all mankind that man was created to work: *Homo nascitur ad laborem, et avis ad volatum* (Job 5:7), man is born to work and the bird to fly' (31 May 1954).

The biblical references could be multiplied. There are some which I must mention – those which remind us that Christ fully practised the divine commandment to work: he spent thirty years living like any other villager in Nazareth, earning a reputation on account of his work – he was simply 'the carpenter's son' (Mt 13:54-55). These thirty years during which Christ worked are echoed in and give meaning to every Christian's ordinary life: 'I don't understand how you can call yourself a Christian and lead such an idle, useless life. Have you forgotten Christ's life of toil?' (Way 356).

Commenting on Monsignor Escrivá's teaching, Fr Alvaro del Portillo has recalled some texts he used to illustrate the divine commandment to work:

> For example, there are the words of Psalm 103, which so wonderfully praise God for his creation and for the harmony which he has disposed in the universe, and the way which all created things – mountains, valleys, waters, animals – obey him: 'Man goes forth to his work and to his labour until the evening' (Ps. 103, 23). Man should work because this is God's will, the law laid

17

down by the Creator several times (cf. Gen. 2:15; 3:23): 'Six days you shall do your work but on the seventh day you shall rest' (Ex. 23:12); 'Whatever your hand finds to do, do it with your might' (Eccl. 9: 10). Our Lord Jesus Christ gave us an example of hard work by his thirty years of hidden life, when he worked as a carpenter (Mark 6:3). And he continued to work: he replied to criticism that he worked [by performing miracles] on the sabbath: 'My Father is working still, and I am working' (John 5:17). Jesus condemns the man who does not put to good use the talent he has received: 'You wicked and slothful servant' (Matt. 25:26). He curses the fig tree because it yields no fruit: 'May no one ever eat fruit from you again. . . . As they passed by in the morning they saw the fig tree withered away to its roots. And Peter remembered and said to him: "Master, look! The fig tree that you cursed has withered" (Mark 11:12 and 20-21). Saint Luke recalls the Creator's commandment: 'There are six days on which work ought to be done' (13:14). Saint Paul insists time and again on the need to work with a right intention: 'Whatever your task, work heartily, as serving the Lord and not men' (Col. 3:23); and exhorts Christians to live a quiet hardworking life (1 Thes 4:11; 2 Thes 3: 12); he gave his disciples a constant example, such that he could boast that 'these hands have ministered to my necessities, and to those who were with me' (Acts 20:34). In this way, with his professional work (Acts 18:3) he supports his companions, teaches them, carries out his apostolate and can say joyfully: 'Are you not my workmanship in the Lord?' (1 Cor 9:1).

Del Portillo concludes:

Many quotations from holy Scripture can be cited to affirm that man has to work because this is God's command. And our founder drew the conclusion – if we can become saints by fulfilling God's will then we can become saints by working (in our ordinary work, in the place where God puts us); and we will be able to lead others towards the same holiness. . . . His doctrine gives back to ordinary work its specific place in the economy of creation and leads to a logical consequence: ordinary work, done to perfection (because that is what God wants), raised to the supernatural order, is a means of sanctification – of Christian perfection – and therefore of apostolate.

The scriptural texts which describe work as a law willed by God already show us work's sanctifying value – for what does becoming holy 18   mean if not doing God's will, identifying oneself with what God wants and therefore with what God *is*? And the texts which report Christ's life of work teach us this in a particularly vivid way.

It's not surprising, then, that the founder of Opus Dei spoke often and eloquently about these years of Christ's life. For example, in a homily given on Christmas Day 1963: 'The fact that Jesus grew up and lived just like us shows us that human existence and all the ordinary activity of men have a divine meaning. No matter how much we may have reflected on all this, we should always be surprised when we think of the thirty years of obscurity which made up the greater part of Jesus' life among men. He lived in obscurity, but, for us, that period is full of light. It illuminates our days and fills them with meaning, for we are ordinary Christians who lead an ordinary life, just like millions of other people all over the world.

'That was the way Jesus lived for thirty years, as "the son of the carpenter" (Mt 13:55). There followed three years of public life, spent among the crowds. People were surprised: "Who is this?" they asked. "Where has he learned these things?" for he was just like them: he had shared the life of ordinary people. He was "the carpenter, the son of Mary" (Mk 6:3). And he was God; he was achieving the redemption of mankind and "drawing all things to himself" (Jn 12:32)' (Christ passing 14).[29]

The founder of Opus Dei then looks at the people in Jesus' circle: at Saint Joseph, who was entrusted with the human care of the Son of God; at the early Christians, those men and women who had known Christ and had lived with the Apostles – and from whom Christians today and of any period of history can draw inspiration. He discovers that all of them work: Saint Joseph, whose life was 'simple, ordinary and normal', full of years of 'work done in God's presence' (Christ passing 44); Saint Peter, a fisherman by occupation and by choice, who whenever the opportunity came up would go back to the nets;[30] Saint Paul who, after leaving Athens, went to Corinth where 'he found a Jew named Aquila, a native of Pontus, lately come from Italy with his wife Priscilla . . . and he went to see them; and because he was of the same trade he stayed with them, and they worked with him for by trade they were tent makers' (Acts 18: 1–3). Paul's hardworking life gave him the authority to denounce idleness and his lesson was admirably taken to heart by the first generations of Christians.[31] The *Didache* gives a graphic example of this when it outlines the attitude which should be adopted to wayfarers: 'If the one who comes to you is a transient visitor, assist him as much as you can, but he may not stay with you more than two days or, if necessary, three. But if he intends to settle among you, and is a craftsman, let him work for his living; if he has no trade or craft, use your judgment in providing for him, so that a follower of Christ will not live idle in your midst'.[32]

Monsignor Escrivá writes with equal force: 'Opus Dei, *operatio Dei*, work of God, requires its members to work: "Cursed is he who does the work of the Lord with slackness', (Jer. 48:10)' (31 May 1954). As he put it in a homily once: 'If anyone among you didn't love work, his own particular job; if he didn't feel sincerely committed to some noble occupation in this world so as to sanctify it, or if he were to lack a professional vocation, then that person would never be able to understand the supernatural substance of what this priest is saying to you, for the very good reason that he would be lacking an indispensable condition for doing so: that of being a worker' (Friends 58).

## Work and 'professional' or 'everyday' work

Monsignor Escrivá's preaching has done a great deal to remind people of Jesus' life of work. This, in itself, is a contribution to the history of spirituality; but we have to go deeper to find the core of Opus Dei's specific contribution in this regard, for work has been and is a central element in other spiritualities, and particularly in monastic life. It is enough to recall the Benedictine motto which weds work and prayer, *ora et labora*,'[33] or Cassian's account of the life of monks in Egypt which tells us that 'giving themselves no rest from work, neither do they ever cease meditation. . . . It would be tedious to enquire whether it is meditation which permits them to consecrate themselves fully to work, or the other way around – constant work which allows them to progress in the ways of the spirit'.[34]

But what is the real function of work in monastic spirituality? When Saint Athanasius relates the life of Saint Anthony Abbot, the first anchorite, he gives us one explanation when he tells how Anthony 'worked with his hands because he had heard it said that "he who does not work, let him not eat". With part of what he made he bought his sustenance; the rest he gave to the poor'.[35]

In addition to this first function of work – really a dual function: to support oneself and also practise charity – monastic writers indicate others which have more to do with asceticism. Cassian, for example, comments on how the monks, as well as doing their work 'with all their soul, offering to God the sacrifice of their hands, also do it scrupulously for two reasons. In the first place, to ensure that the purification acquired in the recital of the psalms and prayers is not contaminated by the enemy while they sleep. . . . The second reason is that when they go back to sleep again, even if there is no shameful imaginations produced by the enemy, even if it is totally pure, sleep causes in the monk a certain natural inertia when he later wakes up; it immerses the mind in an indolent stupor which paralyses him or at least neutralises his efforts during the day'.[36] He elaborates on this in Book X when he describes the vice of laziness or sloth: absence of work gives rise to discontent, permits the body to be overcome by laziness, and causes impatience; it encourages one to wander from one thing to another and leads to inconstancy and dissatisfaction.

In other words, work is seen basically as a means of fighting idleness, the mother of all vices. It is not sought as something good in itself, but simply as an ascetical means. A good example of this largely instrumental view of work (as something done because it is useful but without considering its own intrinsic goodness) is the story of Paul the Hermit who set himself the task of making baskets (though they were no use to him for his maintenance and almsgiving, since he lived off a small plot of land and too far from any inhabited place): at the end of the year he made a heap of the baskets and burned them.[37]

Of course it would be easy to make too much out of this anecdote. Usually monastic work was linked with the environment in which it was set, so that monks in fact performed an important social role. But the fact that this sort of thing happened and has been recorded, because it is seen as being in some way edifying, has a certain significance. It reminds us that the monk is essentially a man who has *left his place*: his spirituality is dominated by the ideal of *contemptus saeculi, fuga mundi* (leaving the world in order to look for God and give oneself to him) and all that derives from this ideal.

Bearing all this in mind we can pick up again our main thread. The spirituality of Opus Dei leads a person to sanctify work but – I should now add – for Opus Dei the word 'work' does not mean something 'physical' (human energies occupied in some concrete task); it is used in the sense of being something which roots a person in the world and in society.

In this connection one of the most significant texts of the founder of Opus Dei runs as follows: 'For us work means dignity of life and a duty imposed by the Creator, since man was actually created *ut operaretur*. Work is a means by which man shares in Creation: and therefore it is not only something very worthy (no matter what form it takes), but it is an instrument for achieving human perfection – earthly perfection and supernatural perfection. In human terms it is a source of progress, 21 civilisation and wellbeing, and Christians have a duty to build the earthly city, in charity towards all men and for their own personal fulfilment' (31 May 1954). As he put it in a homily in 1963: 'Work, all work, bears witness to the dignity of man, to his dominion over creation. It is an opportunity to develop one's personality. It is a bond of union with others, the way to support one's family, a means of aiding in the improvement of the society in which we live and in the progress of all mankind. For a Christian these horizons extend and grow wider. For work is a participation in the creative work of God. When he created man and blessed him, he said: "Be fruitful, multiply, fill the earth, and subdue it. Be masters of the fish of the sea, the birds of heaven and all living animals on the earth" (Gen 1:28). And, moreover, since Christ took it into his hands, work has become for us a redeemed and redemptive reality. Not only is it the background of man's life, it is a means and path of holiness. It is something to be sanctified and some-earth, and subdue it. Be masters of the fish of the sea, the birds of heaven and all living animals on the earth" (Gen 1:28). And, moreover, since Christ took it into his hands, work has become for us a redeemed and redemptive reality. Not only is it the background of man's life, it is a means and path of holiness. It is something to be sanctified and something which sanctifies' (Christ passing 47).[38]

In other words, when Monsignor Escrivá speaks of work and its supernatural implications he is referring to 'professional work and all that work involves in terms of duties of state, obligations and social relationships' (31 May 1954). That is why he rarely uses the bare term 'work' without qualifying it to explain himself better. Thus, he speaks of 'professional' work, 'ordinary' work, 'everyday' work. By this he means a stable way of life, something by which a man earns his living, an extension of his own personality and an expression of his ambitions and talents. It is a way of achieving that solidarity which binds people to one another, of being rooted in temporal society, an activity whose characteristics are dictated by human structures. So, in the spirituality of Opus Dei part of the *divine vocation* is the *human vocation* which it raises – the whole ensemble of particular circumstances: the particular job, the noble aspirations and the generous inclinations which go to make up each person's activity'[39]: our professional calling is not only a part but a principal part of our supernatural vocation.'[40]

Precisely because of this, an indispensable condition for being a member of Opus Dei is that one must not only work but have a job t do in the world: Opus Dei, its founder has said, 'requires its members to work, to have a specific profession or trade – *munus publicum* –

well known to all; because for the members of the Work one's job is a means of sanctification and apostolate' (31 May 1954).[41] It doesn't matter what one's job is but one has to be a worker, to have a specific job. If that is missing, there just is nothing there to be sanctified. 'If anyone thinks that any honest human work, humble or important, cannot lead to holiness and apostolate you can tell him with complete assurance that he does not have a vocation to Opus Dei' (9 January 1932).

Going a step further, it is worth pointing out that all the exhortations and guidelines given by the founder of Opus Dei regarding the value of everyday work are based on Scripture, on deep reflection on God's plan for creation and salvation. In a homily in 1967 he put it this way: 'We must love the world and work and all human things. For the world is good. Adam's sin destroyed the divine balance of creation; but God the Father sent his only Son to re-establish peace, so that we, his children by adoption, might free creation from disorder and reconcile all things to God' (Christ passing 112). And, at greater length, three years later: 'Christ our Lord still wants to save men and the whole of creation — this world of ours which is good, for so it came from God's hands. It was Adam's offence, the sin of human pride, which broke the divine harmony of creation. But God the Father, in the fullness of time, sent his only-begotten Son to take flesh in Mary ever Virgin, through the Holy Spirit, and re-establish peace. In this way, by redeeming man from sin, "we receive adoption as sons" (Gal 4:5). We become capable of sharing the intimacy of God. In this way the new man, the new line of the children of God (cf Rom 6:4-5), is enabled to free the whole universe from disorder, restoring all things in Christ (cf Rom 6:4-5), as they have been reconciled with God (cf Col 1:20)'.[42]

So we are a long way away from a merely ascetical view (work as a remedy for idleness) or a purely ethical one (work as a duty of one's state in life). Work is seen against the background of the very work of creation and it is rooted in the redemption wrought by Christ. That is how it comes to be seen as something sanctifiable and sanctifying. Indeed, it can be seen as an anticipation of the final end of the world, because, thanks to work, it is possible to reestablish (though in the limited way possible in this present era) that harmony of creation which we will fully enjoy when history comes to an end, when the new heaven and the new earth come about.[43]

## Work in the history of spirituality

The dogmatic perspectives I have just referred to are deeply rooted in the Gospels; and the Fathers and Doctors of the Church have comment-    23 ed on them, although generally without spelling out the sanctifiable and sanctifying value of work. Why is this? Historically, what are the reasons for this silence? Again, I think, it has to do with the decisive new orientation of theology from the time of monasticism onwards: not just because spiritual theology's attention became centred on other questions but also because, since it looked on work mainly as an ascetical device, as a manual exercise to keep the spirit alert, theological reflection was rather blinkered: it could not be expected to notice very much. A fully rounded theological view of work must start off with a total notion of work and therefore it cannot just look at manual work: it has to look also at the division of roles which social structurisation implies; at the problem of the meaning of history; at the actual content of the secular, lay vocation; etc.[44]

Let us not forget that, from the time of early monasticism onwards, the religious state has undergone a steady evolution, taking in a series of rich new contributions – distinct in many respects from the original monasticism. In fact at certain points the subject of work did begin to take shape – but it went no further than that. It is an interesting process, which we might look at briefly.

The monastic ideals has as its central point of reference the personal search for evangelical perfection; it is not expressly concerned with a direct apostolate, with the care of souls. In the *Rule* of Saint Benedict, for example, there is not a single reference to the apostolic activities of the monk outside the monastery. Indeed, after covering in chapter IV the norms of life which the monk should practise, Saint Benedict concludes: 'The place where we should diligently practise these things is the precinct of the monastery'.[45]

It would be a gross misunderstanding of the origin and history of monasticism to conclude from this that apostolate is absent from the monastic ideal: it is there not only theologically speaking (the virtue of charity unites the love of God and the love of men) but also from a sociological point of view. But it is not so much the monk as an individual as the monastery itself that does the apostolate: the reputation of the heroic life of the monks and the very character of the monastery, so often built on the top of a mountain, are a focus of spiritual radiation which influences everything around and moves men to a more sincere Christian life.

As time goes on, the picture changes and there is a growing connection between monasticism and pastoral care. From the very beginning, in both East and West, it was commonplace for monks to be raised to the episcopate, and the missionary activity of monks, like Augustine,

Columbanus, Boniface, Cyril and Methodius, and so many others, attracted new peoples to the faith. In 1096 there was an interesting legislative development when the Council of Nimes, called by Urban II who needed the monks' support for his reforms, proclaimed that monks could devote themselves to the pastoral ministry since they were fully equipped for that work.[46]

The biggest changes came with the rise of the mendicant orders, Franciscans and Dominicans. Their conception of a religious life in which stability took second place, and the setting up of a centralised hierarchy, made possible a new juridical type – that of the friar, whose *principal* activity (unlike the monk's) is to go preaching from city to city and town to town.

In the sixteenth century two new factors had sweeping effects on all Christian life: religious unity was broken by schism, and the new geographical discoveries revealed peoples whom Christ's word had not yet reached. These influences helped the rise of the regular clergy – Theatines, Somaschi, Barnabites, Jesuits. These new religious institutes combined the priesthood and the life of perfection with a more flexible and efficient organisation of apostolate – centralised government, absence of the monastic habit and of choir, and so forth. In other words, the preaching of the word was done closer to, nearer the midst of the Christian people whom these religious helped live up to their calling, or among pagans, whom they wished to bring to the Faith.

In later centuries we find an increase in societies of religious – men or women – which grew from this desire to do an ever more effective apostolate adapted to the needs of the times. And, more and more religious institutes arose with the purpose not of preaching but of doing charitable, welfare or educational work very varied in type. Two juridical devices helped this evolution: the congregations of simple vows, and societies of common life without vows.

The main feature of this whole development was an ever closer relationship between the life of perfection and apostolic work in one form or other.

All this is very important but it doesn't bring us any nearer to affirming the value of everyday work or the full content of the lay or secular vocation: in fact it really goes off in the opposite direction. Even the very social structure of those centuries – first feudal, then divided into estates in which individuals mattered not in their own right but as members or components of the estate to which they belonged: even this played its part in making it difficult to see the sanctifying value of the work each person did. At this time society had a very hierarchical 25 structure based on inheritance, so that access to influential positions depended primarily not on personal competence but on family connection. This permitted an attitude which considered work as dishonourable or as something not worth talking about. The message of the sanctification of work is more easily understood in an era like our own when the main element of social diversification and structurisation is the professional competence of the individual. But the main reason for not giving everyday work its importance was the development which I have been outlining.

Thus we find that monastic spirituality spoke of manual work done in the cloister; although carried out with a completely different approach it had a certain *material* similarity to work done in the world; this left the way open to pose the problem of the sanctification of that work in the world.[47] Yet as time went by manual work ceased to be the object of attention: ecclesiastical tasks came to be considered as the only really sanctifying ones. This in effect closed the way to recognition of the sanctifying value of everyday work; and it remained closed for a long time. (We should not forget the value of ecclesiastical work, the result of an often heroic effort and always the opportunity for a real exercise of virtue. Even a superficial knowledge of the history of the Church or a minimum experience of apostolate in our own times shows the marvellous work which has been and is being done by so many secular priests and religious men and women devoted to the care of souls or educational or welfare activities. All that I am saying is that there is more to life than ecclesiastical roles, and a spiritual theology is inadequate if it does not *also* affirm the value of everyday work done by an ordinary citizen in the middle of the world — work with which he supports himself and his family, serves the society of which he forms part, etc.)

The thirteenth century marks a crucial point, because it features the polemic between the new mendicant orders, and secular clergy and representatives of some monastic institutions. The friars were being critisized for not doing manual work which had been a feature of monastic tradition: therefore they tried to show that the search for evangelical perfection was compatible with not working manually, living on alms rather than earning one's living by the work of one's hands. Reflecting on their own spirituality and faced with the need to break the rigid link between work and manual occupation, they were in a position to elaborate a more complete theology of work as an integral element in the life of man. But it did not turn out that way: the theologians of the mendicants only went so far as to deal with objections by stating that manual work was not something binding on all. They did not go into the whole question of work; in fact they dealt with work in a rather negative way.

This even happens in Saint Thomas Aquinas – which you would not expect, given the importance he gives to the virtues of magnanimity and magnificence; the depth of his analysis of art as an intellectual virtue directed to perfecting the work one wants to do, etc[48]; if you read the chapters on this subject in his *Contra impugnantes Dei cultum et religionem* in which he replies to those who criticise mendicants for not doing manual work, it is clear that he too goes no further than this rather negative view of work.[49] We find the same sort of thing in Saint Bonaventure and his school.[50]

An interesting example of the post-Bonaventure outlook is the description in the *Meditationes vitae Christi* of Jesus' years at Nazareth:

> The Lord Jesus left the company and conversation of the people and went into a synagogue – that is to say, a church – and spent there a time in prayer, in the lowest place. On returning home he was with his mother and sometimes helped her and Joseph and walked among the people, coming and going, as if he saw no one. The people were amazed to see such a fine young man with apparently nothing to do. . . . They were amazed and they made fun of him saying: 'He is a dead loss, an idiot, good for nothing; he is stupid, he is mad, he can't even learn the ABC'. . . . Consider then this family blessed as none other . . . Joseph, an old man, earning whatever he could by his work, and the mother earning by sewing and weaving and doing the many other tasks in the house. And she prepared meals for her son and Joseph and did other like things that had to be done, because they had no other servants. Therefore, have compassion on her, seeing her obliged to work laboriously with her hands. Have compassion also on Jesus who helped her faithfully and tried to do all he could. Here is he of whom the Gospel says: 'I came to serve, not to be served'.
>
> [The people] poured scorn on him [Jesus] and jeered at him and said: 'Who is this?, is he not the son of a carpenter?' And they said of him other vile things of this type.[51]

Mention should also be made of other developments in the middle ages which refer in a way to the sanctification of work even if they were provided with no theological theory. For example, the military orders – and especially the confraternities, which were very closely connected with the professional guilds, to the extent that they even ran insurance schemes to cover illness, poverty, burials, etc. It would be interesting to investigate how far the intellectual evolution I have referred to influenced the development of these confraternities. However, even if these confraternities pointed to a positive evaluation of work (shown particularly in the figure of the patron saint, chosen precisely because some virtue or scene of his life had a connection with the trade entrusted to him) there was still no well-defined spiritual background. Their activities, apart from the welfare ones just mentioned, were limited to public worship (processions, solemn masses, suffrages for the dead, etc.); they did not give the members in any direct way an ascetical or doctrinal training which would bring them to sanctify their work as such. Much research has been done into the medieval corporations from the viewpoint of economic history but there has been little theological research in this field.[52]

In the great medieval writers there are of course some fruitful and positive ideals and insights on this subject but in general they concentrate on other questions. The fact is that as time went on writers steadily paid less attention to the subject of work. Among the spiritual writers at the end of the middle ages the Flemish school occupied a prominent place. Its inspiration came from Ruysbroeck and out of it came one of the most widely-read of all ascetical books, *The Imitation of Christ.* The author mentions work early on when he deals with the life of the first monks and hermits who 'after a day of hard work, must still be long over their praying – as if work itself had meant rest, for a moment, from mental prayer'[53] but in fact his assessment of work is much more negative than that of the fathers of the desert. Here I need give only the following example: 'He [man] must eat and drink, sleep and wake, labour and rest – all these natural needs have their claim on him, and it makes a devout soul feel wretched and harassed; why can't he be clear of it all, beyond the reach of sin'.[54] Possibly this negative approach is responsible for a theoretical and semantic evolution which one notices running right through the *Imitation*: the opposition between idleness and work of which Scripture and the early monks speak tends to become an opposition between idleness and ascetical struggle; that is, idleness is taken to mean lack of dedication to the interior life, and work is the effort that the ascetical struggle requires.[55]

Roughly the same can be said about the spiritual movement begun by the canons of Winsdesheim and continued by books devoted to describing methods of prayer, such as Cisneros' *Ejercitatorio de la vida espiritual*[56] and, following on this, the *Spiritual Exercises* of Saint Ignatius, who in fact lived for a time in the Abbey of Montserrat where

Cisneros' influence was very strong. Significantly, when the word 'work' appears in the *Exercises* it does not mean ordinary everyday work; in the singular Saint Ignatius used 'work' to mean ascetical struggle, self-giving to Christ; in the plural it means difficulties, sorrows and obstacles. The second use is the most frequent.[57]

However, in the period of humanism and the renaissance we find there is a renewed interest in the subject of human work. On the one hand you get various humanists – Thomas More and Erasmus, for example – very keen to ensure that Christian spirit and thought not be the exclusive affair of the cloister: they try to make it influence the new secular environments which are emerging. And, on the other hand, the spirit of exploration and adventure which was such a feature of the period meant that more importance was given to human activity in so far as it was directed to imposing itself on the world: true, there was the danger that this could lead to a neo-paganism, but in certain cases the development was inspired by Christian faith. The crisis provoked by Protestantism prevented all this from developing in a calm, fruitful way; later authors do have some useful insights but they lack an over-view of the whole question.

Both Luther and Calvin spoke of professions and of work (which Luther even described as 'service of the Lord') and, taking up the teachings of the great medieval doctors, they related work to the work of creation: 'God-at-work continues his work through man-at-work'. But neither managed to discover the sanctifying value of work; in fact they were a real obstacle to its discovery. Their view of original sin as the absolute corruption of human nature, and their attempt to deny that human activity, even that done in the state of grace, had any merit in God's sight, all closed the door to any progress on this subject. Luther's idea of work as service and Calvin's statements about the value of work as a sign of predestination had a very widespread influence in their time. But they both set up a dualism – on the one hand, the *sola fides*, 'faith alone', which justifies, together with predestination; and, on the other, work seen as a service to man, but regarded as having no value in God's sight; and this dualism led to a severe dichotomy between an individualistic pietism on the one hand and a humanism without theological roots on the other. We can hear the echo of this even today.

Catholic theology in the renaissance and baroque periods avoided these extremes; in the field of the philosophy of law it was very productive and it seemed to be heading in the right direction. But it became contaminated by a kind of aristocratic ideal which had little use for technical and business work. It also, became trapped in a narrow 29 moralism which was incapable of grasping the value of human work. A desire to criticise the errors of Luther and Calvin, and later on to correct the excesses of illuminism and quietism, gave rise to an acute wariness of anything tinged with mysticism. It is not surprising, therefore, for Melchor Cano, for example, to affirm expressly that lay people cannot reach the height of Christian perfection and to oppose vigorously those who published books in the vernacular to direct lay people along the ways of prayer.[58]

Certainly, all the authors of the sixteenth century and later stressed the importance of one's choice of state in life and of one's duties of state but this did not bring them to study and evaluate the activity carried out in each state. Rather, it led them to develop a theory of states, inspired by Roman law doctrine on status, which was used by Saint Thomas in the *Summa* and was definitely elaborated by Suarez in his treatise *De Religione*.[59] This theory was based on a rigid classification of persons; the subject of the call to holiness is fitted into this structure — and this makes it very difficult to affirm the riches of Christian vocation in *the world*.

At the beginning of the seventeenth century an attempt was made to correct the excesses of anti-mysticism and once again direct the faithful along the ways of prayer and full Christian life. The most outstanding figure in this movement was Saint Francis de Sales who writes in the prologue to his *Introduction to the Devout Life*: 'Almost all those authors who have hitherto treated of devotion have had in view the instruction of persons wholly withdrawn from the world, or they have taught a kind of devotion that leads to this absolute retirement. My intention is to instruct those who live in towns, in families, or at court. By their condition they are obliged to lead, as to outward appearances, an ordinary life'.[60]

The works of Saint Francis de Sales and of later writers who followed his example did a great deal of good to ordinary Christians and were an effective help to their piety. Yet they did not reopen the discussion of the supernatural value of terrestrial realities: the theory of states had become the only accepted framework for interpreting anything to do with the aspiration of holiness, and all these various spiritual movements involving laity were eventually incorporated into the evolution of the religious state.[61]

On the other hand — and Cardinal Luciani has pointed this out — if the holy bishop of Geneva realised the need for Christians living in the world to be invited to holiness, he usually 'suggests the same practical means as used by religious, but with suitable modifications.'[62] In other words he did not understand the core of lay spirituality i.e. that it consists in a spiritual attitude which takes fully into account the secular experience of the person concerned.

A clear example of this real incapacity to understand secular values is given by the fact that when, in the spiritual theology of those centuries, reference is made to work in the sense of human activity, it is a reference to activities of an ecclesiastical type, not to everyday work in the world. Or, rather, both are referred to but the former are mentioned to show how they have supernatural roots, whereas the latter – secular occupations – are referred to in the context of providing an obstacle to the search for holiness.[63]

## The difference between 'being in the world' and 'approaching the world'

We have been looking at the development of the religious state, seeing how it is characterised by an ever clearer perception of the link between the call to holiness, and apostolate: for this reason it moves closer to the world, which it wants to evangelise. And we have also seen how, due to a complex series of factors, this development does not lead to a recognition of the sanctifying value of work but rather goes in the other direction.

However, we have not yet exhausted the richness acquired by the religious state since its monastic beginnings: there is a last stage, which we must refer to, just to make sure that it does not confuse our understanding of the lay and secular vocation. In this stage religious become so involved in life in the world that it might appear that the religious life had actually blended completely with life in the world. Can this be true?

The suppression of the religious orders during the period of the French Revolution led to the founding of associations with the same spirit as those orders but without their external appearance. Other factors which encouraged this development were the desire to extend the apostolate to environments where the habit or soutane would be unwelcome; eagerness to recover the working masses for the Church (this led to reflection on the relationship between poverty and work);[64] and the influence of spiritualities (such as Charles de Foucauld's) based the idea of witness, in the sense of presence. The new feature of this form of the religious state was that religious go right into the world; and so we find a religious spirituality which refers to work not simply as a physical reality but in the sense of earthly occupations.

But, does it refer to these occupations in a secular way, I mean, with the same outlook as the ordinary Christian, the layman, looks at them? It is worth remembering that although the religious vocation or state has evolved substantially and radically over the centuries it has kept its basic theology. All and each of its forms have maintained the attitude which gave rise to it in the first place – the attitude of distinction and opposition with respect to the world – the world in the sense not of sin or evil inclinations but earthly society, ordinary civil life.

At the beginning the religious ideal for the search for holiness put a marked emphasis on material distance from that world; in later forms it emphasises a physical approach to it but it always keeps that distance as a vital attitude, as an outlook. You can see this in the very expressions used to describe the spirituality of the newest associations: they speak of living *like* others, of acting *in the same way as* ordinary citizens, of *joining* those who work, etc. And, also, the centre of their spiritual life is placed away from that world; the interior life is nourished from the cloister. Saint Jerome's celebrated phrase, 'the city is for me a prison; the wilderness a paradise'[65], is still the rule of religious spirituality, which seeks in the solitude of the cloister the strength to give content to its presence in apostolic work. 'To meet the essentially theological purpose of all religious life', the Secretary of the Congregation of Religious, Monsignor Philippe, commented in 1963, 'they create in their houses a tranquil atmosphere, aimed at protecting, fostering and perfecting the interior life of their own religious. From here they go out to serve their neighbour, to here they return to devote themselves to God'.[66]

The same spirit is to be found in the style of life of various Secular Institutes and other similar associations which, using ordinary dress during the working day, change to a habit when they return to their houses; and there is even the case of members of one 'Secular Institute' taking public vows, like religious.[67]

Finally, the apostolate of these later religious aims at bringing the presence of the Church into the world, into secular life; and this they certainly do but they make present something which comes from outside and reminds us of our duties; in sum it is a testimony of authority rather than of friendship. One might say that in a sociologically distinct environment theirs is a function similar to that performed by the monastery in relation to the countryside around it.[68]

Everyone knows that in the years since 1965 many religious institutes have severely changed their lifestyle to such an extent that it is difficult to say exactly where they will go in the future. I cannot attempt to go into that here; all I am saying is that we find the religious state evolving in some way or other towards rapproachment to the world.

Let us now turn to Opus Dei. One of the first things we can notice is how careful the founder was to point out that if the last stages of the development of the religious state coincided, timewise, with the birth of Opus Dei that was the end of the coincidence since the two phenomena obeyed completely different inspirations.

In 1968, in an interview, he said: 'I consider the religious vocation a blessed one and one which the Church needs, and anyone who did not venerate that vocation would not have the spirit of the Work. But it is not my vocation, nor that of the members of Opus Dei. You can say that; in coming to Opus Dei, each and every member has come *on the explicit condition of not changing his state in life*' (Conversations 62). Many years earlier he had put it even more forcefully: 'God has not given us the vocation of religious . . . We are not religious and – to put it graphically, even though the hypothesis is absurd – there is no authority on earth which could oblige us to be religious: natural law forbids it, as does divine positive law, and christian morality and ecclesiastical law: for we have given ourselves to God expressly on the condition of not being religious' (19 March 1954).

On the same occasion, after referring to the development of the religious state he added that the ideas and standards used to assess the history of religious life could not in any way be applied to interpret the birth and life of Opus Dei; 'here we have a completely different phenomenon, for we are not secularised religious but genuine laypeople who do not look for the life of evangelical perfection proper to religious but for Christian perfection in the world, each in his own state in life and in the exercise of his profession or trade. Anyone unable to see beyond the classical moulds of the life of perfection will not understand the structure of the Work. The members of Opus Dei are not religious (to take one example) who, full of holy zeal, work as lawyers, doctors, engineers, manual labourers etc.; they are simply lawyers, doctors, engineers, manual labourers etc., who have a great interest in their work and the outlook characteristic of it, for whom this work, and naturally their whole life, acquires a fuller meaning when it is directed completely to God and to the salvation of souls'.[69]

In this 1948 article Monsignor Escrivá goes right back to the very beginnings of the Church in his search for historical precedents for Opus Dei. He goes to those first Christians who felt in their souls the desire to put into practice, as far as human nature elevated by grace can do so, the ideals outlined in the Gospel – and without leaving the world: back to those early ascetics who stayed in the middle of the society of their time, living with their families, involved in ordinary occupations, the same as everyone else.[70] Indeed, Monsignor Escrivá was always talking about the early Christians. 'Just as observant religious', he wrote in the thirties, 'are eager to know how the first of their order or congregation lived, so as to have their model to follow, you too, Christian gentleman, should also seek to know and imitate the lives of the disciples of Jesus, who knew Peter and Paul and John, and all but witnessed the Death and Resurrection of the Master' (Way 925).[71] And in 1967, when an American journalist asked him what movements or associations could Opus Dei be compared to he replied: 'If you want a point of comparison, the easiest way to understand Opus Dei is to consider the life of the early Christians' (Conversations 24).[72]

It would be a mistake to regard all this as a series of historical or legal niceties, for this whole matter has important implications for spiritual theology and particularly for an understanding of the place which work and the whole gamut of human activities and realities should have in the spiritual life of the ordinary Christian.

The evolution of the religious state can be compared with a movement from outside to inside: something, existing independently of the world, and having a raison d'être which implies a going away from the world, now turns its attention to the world. In the case of Opus Dei, on the contrary, everything is done where one was and where one continues to be – in the middle of the world. So, if the religious experience can be described as 'approaching the world' or 'a presence in the world' i.e. using expressions which semantically imply that one was previously outside or separate from that world which one is approaching or becoming present in, the experience of Opus Dei must be defined as 'being of the world', i.e. it excludes at the root any separation, any distance, even if only temporary or psychological in character. 'Opus Dei contains within itself Christians of every walk of life, men and women, single and married, who being in the middle of the world or, better, being of the world – for they are ordinary lay people – aspire, by divine vocation, to Christian perfection'.[73]

'Our vocation means precisely that our secular condition, our ordinary work, our situation in the world, is our only way of sanctification and apostolate. It is not that we use that secular occupation to 'cover' an apostolic work; rather, it is simply the occupation which we would have, had we the misfortune to leave our vocation. We are, my sons and daughters, people in the street. And when we work in temporal things we do so because that is our place, that is where we find Jesus Christ, that is where our calling has left us' (19 March 1954).[74]

'I hope', Monsignor Escrivá said in 1968, 'that the time will come when the phrase "the Catholics are penetrating all sectors of society" will go out of circulation because everyone will have realized that it is a clerical expression. In any event, it is quite inapplicable to the apostolate of Opus Dei. The members of the Work have no need to "penetrate" the temporal sector for the simple reason that they are ordinary citizens, the same as their fellow citizens, and so they are *there already*'. And, a little earlier in the same interview: 'One cannot speak of adaptation to the world or to modern society. No one adapts himself to what is part and parcel of himself: with respect to what is proper to himself he simply *is*.'[75]

The dogmatic aspects of this subject, which we touched on earlier, are also relevant here. In underlining the sovereign effectiveness of the Redemption they show that Christianity is not something set alongside the world, adapting itself as if coming from outside and therefore failing to establish deep, living relationships with the world. No: Christianity vivifies the world from within. Grace is, true, a new life, a spontaneous gratuitous gift of God; but precisely because of that – because it is a life communicated by him who is the source of our existence – grace involves our whole being, from its innermost core, affecting every aspect of our life.

Christian dogma proclaims that man is called to share in God's own intimate life – in a full way at the end of time but also now, albeit in a partial way, through grace. This makes it possible both to go away from the world and bear witness to the eschatological side of things, *and* to sanctify oneself in the context of this world by virtue of grace. The word 'world' has various meanings; two of these are particularly relevant to this essay: (1) world in the socio-anthropological sense i.e. world as the whole ensemble of institutions, relationships and involvements where people ordinarily live; and (2) the biblio-soteriological world, or world as a situation in which sin reigns, world in need of redemption. Confusion between these two meanings gives rise to serious misunderstandings in regard to our present subject. It is quite obvious that every Christian must leave the world in the second sense – but not in the first sense (unless God so indicates to a person by means of a special calling), for that world is not in itself sin but rather something that is capable of being sanctified through the action of grace.[76]

All this implies that the ordinary Christian who by God's will is in the world does not see himself as a stranger here but as someone who is living in a place which is rightfully his as man and also as Christian. The secular, practice of Christianity is something which comes from the core of the Catholic faith: it is an affirmation of the original goodness of the world and a proclamation of the healing and divinising effectiveness of grace and therefore of the sanctifiable and sanctifying value of the world (and of work, as a basic element of it) provided that it is brought into the forefront of our effort to live a Christian life.

# III OPUS DEI &
# SECULAR SPIRITUALITY:

## WORK, HOLINESS AND APOSTOLATE IN
## THE MIDDLE OF THE WORLD

Up to now we have been trying to locate the spirituality of Opus Dei in an historical context: now we will look at it in its own right, using some of the same themes and adding others, for Monsignor Escrivá's preaching does not just proclaim the call to sanctification in the middle of the world: it also gives a very tangible account of what this ideal pre-supposes and implies.

We could approach this either systematically or through its sources. By systematically I mean starting off with the dogmatic principles and statements on which a spirituality is based and then going on to look at its spiritual, ascetical and other implications. In the case of the founder of Opus Dei this would mean analysing his deep understanding of the mystery of Christ and what he had to say about awareness of being children of God; then showing, as deriving from it, a Christian evalu-ation of the world and of earthly realities, and then going on to explore the panorama of a life of holiness and apostolate which is completely secular and lay in style.[77] By a 'source' approach I mean one which aims at showing how Monsignor Escrivá's interior life and preach-ing developed, and showing also how he got his spirit across to those men and women, ordinary Christians, whom he addressed in his apos-tolate.

I am going to follow the latter method, for we are dealing here with expressions of spiritual and apostolic life and 'in this order of realities', as Monsignor Escrivá has himself said, 'first comes life, the lived pastoral phenomenon. Then law, which usually grows up out of custom. Finally, the theological theory, which is worked out on the basis of the lived phenomenon. And, from the very beginning, doctrine and practice must be carefully watched to ensure that neither the life nor the law nor the theory stray away from the faith and moral teaching of Jesus Christ' (19 March 1954).

The spirit of Opus Dei was not the result of theological reflection;

instead, it came from real life actualised by the Spirit who is life. Only later was it subjected to reflection and analysis. So it is reasonable that in the earlier works of its founder the aspect most clearly delineated is that of a life of prayer, holiness and apostolate in the middle of the world, in one's ordinary work. Behind all this was the whole dogmatic side of things which Monsignor Escrivá began to comment upon in more and more depth as time went on.

Of course, he had to open up whole new ways, because the universal call to holiness and the sanctifiable and sanctifying character of earthly realities were not being preached in the 1920's and later. Thus on 2 October 1962, the thirty-fourth anniversary of Opus Dei, Monsignor Escrivá could comment as follows: 'Did the Work really begin on 2 October 1928? Yes, my son, it really began on 2 October 1928. From that moment on I hadn't a minute's "peace". . . . I was twenty six years old, I had God's grace – and good humour: nothing else. But just as we write with a pen, our Lord writes with the leg of a table, so that people can see that it is he who is doing the writing: that is what is so incredible, that is what is so wonderful. All the theological and ascetical doctrine had to be worked out – and the juridical doctrine as well. I had to bridge a gap of centuries: there was nothing to go on. The whole Work, humanly speaking, was a crazy idea.' It was his faithfulness to the light and mission he received in October 1928 that made it possible for this crazy idea to stop being a crazy idea and become a reality, and for his teachings to become generally accepted doctrine.

## Being of the world and the universal call to holiness

How did this preaching of the founder of Opus Dei start? Who was it aimed at? We have already answered this question: at ordinary Christians taken up with the normal things people do – everyday work, social or university involvements, the day to day events of family life. . . . Being of the world is not, remember, an objective, a goal: it is a presupposition. In the spirituality of Opus Dei there is nothing which speaks of distance or separation from the world: it is a spirituality which looks straight at the Christian living among temporal structures, the Christian whose occupation is ordinary work, whose everyday life goes on in the same framework as everyone else's: a spirituality which looks at that Christian precisely in order to help him discover the divine meaning of the setting he finds himself in. Therefore, the effect
38    produced by Monsignor Escrivá's method could be described as 'dis-

covering oneself by being a Christian'.[78] That is really what he wanted to do: he wanted to provoke in his listeners, inserted as they were in the most diverse secular occupations, an awareness that God was calling them, that God expected an answer of them — an answer which had to be given through all the ordinary things which went to make up their lives — and would continue to make up their lives.

'What amazes you seems natural to me: that God has sought you out in the practice of your profession. That is how he sought the first, Peter and Andrew, James and John, beside their nets; and Matthew, sitting in the custom-house. . . ' And — wonder of wonders! — Paul, in his eagerness to destroy the seed of the Christians' (Way 799). And there he has sought you out, we can add, using other texts of his, to help you realise the true meaning of the world you are living in.

The founder of Opus Dei, when speaking of a Christian's vocation (of that moment when a person recognises God's will for him or her) has always given special emphasis to the element of light and lightenment that is involved, while also giving due recognition to elements of invitation and impulse which vocation implies. Probably one reason is that seen from a secular perspective this is the key feature: vocation in the context of earthly reality is not a call to leave the place one is in but rather an invitation to live out the very same existence in a new way — as a consequence of a light which allows one to appreciate that this existence has divine dimensions which previously had been hidden.[79] 'Vocation', said Monsignor Escrivá on 9 January 1932, 'is a new view of life; it is as if a light had been lit inside us'. 'Vocation' as he put it in a homily in 1963, 'discloses to us the meaning of our existence. It means being convinced, through the light of faith, of the reason for our life on earth. Our life, the present, past and future, acquires a new dimension, a depth we did not perceive before. All happenings and events now fall into their true perspective: we understand where God is leading us, and we feel ourselves borne along by this task entrusted to us. God draws us from the shadows of our ignorance, our groping through history, and, no matter what our occupation in the world, he calls us with a strong voice, as he once called Peter and Andrew: "Follow me and I will make you fishers of men" (Mt 4:19)' (Christ passing 45).[80]

This divine light, if accepted by the human heart, involves a deep change in a person's interior, a remaking of mind and will, centering them on God. But in a lay person, in someone living in the world, in an ordinary Christian, all this takes place right where he is, without giving up his profession or trade, without changing his ordinary lifestyle.

Rather, feeling more radically linked to the world as a consequence of the new riches the light of vocation has shown to lie there.

A whole series of Monsignor Escrivá's texts refer to this experience. Some go back to the early days when he had to correct the tendency – common in many quarters – to identify vocation with religious vocation and therefore with an invitation to leave the world. Thus, echoing Saint Paul's words 'Brothers, let each of you remain before God in the position in which he was called' (2 Cor 7:24), he warns people about what he calls the 'madness of leaving your place'. As he put it, on 1 April 1934, for example, 'We don't take anyone out of his place. Each of you stays in the place and social position in the world which is yours. From there, without the madness of leaving your environment, you will give light and energy to so many people! . . . without losing your own energy and your own light, through faith in and through the grace of Jesus Christ, "in which we stand and rejoice awaiting the glory of the sons of God" (Rom 5:2)'.[o1]
of the sons of God" (Rom 5:2)'.[81] 'Without taking anyone out of his place we have come to elevate all human occupations' (31 May 1954). 'Rejoice, when you see others working in good apostolic activities. And ask God to grant them abundant grace and that they may respond to that grace. Then, you, on your way: convince yourself that it's the only way for you' (Way 965).[82]

In the same context we can put some other quotations which call on people not to be escapist but to focus on ordinary life. 'A missionary. – You dream of being a missionary. Another Francis Xavier . . . and you long to conquer an empire for Christ. Japan, China, India, Russia . . . the peoples of the North of Europe, or America, or Africa, or Australia? Stir up that fire in your heart, that hunger for souls. But don't forget that you are more of a missionary "obeying". Geographically distant from those apostolic fields, you work both "here" and "there": don't you – like Xavier – feel your arm tired after administering baptism to so many?' (Way 315). 'You talk of dying "heroically". Do you not think that it is more "heroic" to die a bourgeois death, in a good bed, unnoticed . . . but to die of love-sickness?' (Way 743).

Sometimes, when calling people to *real life*, getting them to give up their day dreams, he used an expression "mistica ojalatería': 'mystical wishful thinking', he said, led them to be indecisive, it sapped their energy. As he put it in a homily in 1967: 'Stop dreaming. Leave behind false idealisms, fantasies, and what I usually call mystical wishful thinking: If only I hadn't married, If only I hadn't this profession, If only I were healthier, If only I were young, If only I were old . . . . Instead turn seriously to the most material and immediate reality, which is where our Lord is: "Look at my hands and my feet", said the risen Jesus, "be assured that it is myself; touch me and see; a spirit has not flesh and bones, as you see that I have" (Lk 24:39).'[83]

The expression 'mystical wishful thinking' has two sides to it: on the one hand it denounces escapism which leads a person to elude the real demands of the Christian vocation; on the other it affirms that Christian vocation can and therefore should be followed in the middle of the world. If his words presuppose that he is addressing men and women of the world, their aim is to open up for them the entire panorama of promises and demands which the Gospel contains. Ordinary Christians, being of the world, loving the world, should also realise that they have been chosen by God, called to the community of the saints, taken not out of the world but out of sin, as Christ put it in his priestly prayer: 'I do not pray that you should take them out of the world, but that you should keep them from evil' (Jn 17:15). 'Be men and women of the world, but don't be worldly men and women,' the founder of Opus Dei had very neatly put it in *The Way* (939).

In fact, his oral and written preaching reflects, with great force, all the central demands of Christianity: sacramental life as the source of all human living, confidence in grace which heals man's weakness, the call to humility, awareness of the central position of the Cross, the invitation to an unconditional self surrender: 'Jesus isn't satisfied "going halves": he wants the lot' (Way 155)[84]; insistence on prayer as an intimate and constant dialogue with God, etc., etc. And giving all this its ultimate meaning, he affirms the absolute perfection of God as something which makes everything else small beer, as the supreme good which the heart should tend towards, with no holding back: 'How little a life is to offer to God!' (Way 420). 'Consider what is most beautiful and most noble on earth, what pleases the mind and the other faculties, and what delights the flesh and the senses. And the world, and the other worlds that shine in the night: the whole universe. Well this, along with all the follies of the heart satisfied, is worth nothing, is nothing and less than nothing compared . . . with this God of mine! – of yours! Infinite treasure, pearl of great price, humbled, become a slave, reduced to the form of a servant in the stable where he chose to be born, in Joseph's workshop, in his passion and in his ignominious death . . . and in the madness of Love which is the blessed Eucharist' (Way 432).

God is, and Monsignor Escrivá never lets us forget it, our last end – our one and only end or purpose, if we take that word in its deepest meaning – to whom all our actions should be addressed. 'If life's purpose were not to give glory to God, how contemptible, how hateful it would be.' 'Give "all" the glory to God. "Squeeze" out each one of your actions with your will aided by grace, so that there remains in them nothing that smacks of human pride, or self-complacency' (Way 783, 784). And, in language which takes us to the opposite pole from any kind of naturalism: 'If you lose the supernatural meaning of your life, your charity will be philanthropy; your purity, decency; your mortification, stupidity; your discipline, a whip; and all your works, fruitless' (Way 291).

We should not be surprised therefore that this supernatural panorama is governed by a statement that the layman should aspire not to a mediocre, languid holiness adapted to his situation: on the contrary, he should aim at the highest, at an heroic, holiness: 'Your duty is to sanctify yourself. Yes, even you. Who thinks that this task is only for priests and religious? To everyone, without exception, our Lord said: "Be ye perfect, as my heavenly Father is perfect"' (Way 291). The Christian, the layman, who works in secular occupations, who lives in what has come to be called the world of the profane: he also should feel urged by God, called to the perfection of charity: 'Lord: may I have due measure in everything . . . except in Love' (Way 427).

All this – I should stress – addressed to people in the world and fully aware of being of the world – not giving up earthly tasks but rather devoting themselves fully to those tasks. Being of the world and being Christian, being of the world and being called to full intimacy with God: there is no contradiction, these things are perfectly compatible. 'The members of Opus Dei', Monsignor Escrivá said on 24 March 1930, 'live an ordinary life, the same life as others of their profession and social environment. In this work they must live an ordered charity and have a genuine desire to do their work perfectly, for love's sake; and they must also live in harmony with all men, to lead them "in season and out of season" (2 Tim 4:2), with the Lord's help and with human elegance, to a Christian life and even to Christian perfection in the world; and this must be combined with a loved and lived personal poverty. My sons know that work can sanctify oneself and others, for Opus Dei is work of God. They feel the need to understand everyone, so as to serve everyone, knowing that they are sons of our Father God who is in heaven, uniting active and contemplative life in a way which becomes second nature, for the spirit of the Work requires this and God's grace helps those who generously serve him in this divine vocation'. Twenty years later the Holy See, in one of the decrees of approval given to Opus Dei, echoed this when it pointed out that the members of

Opus Dei 'carry out with the greatest diligence all honourable professions; and however profane these be they try always to sanctify them through a constantly-renewed purity of intention, with the desire of growing in interior life, with a continuous and joyful self-denial, with the sacrifice of hard, persevering work which should be perfect in all its dimensions'.[85]

So, the member of Opus Dei, an ordinary Christian among ordinary Christians, is not called to a mediocre holiness, to an impoverished holiness (I used that theologically monstrous phrase to make my point) but to the only holiness possible: that which derives from identification with Christ. 'We desire holiness', Monsignor Escrivá said in 1954, 'that Christian perfection which is within the reach of all: we are people of the world, men and women in the street, ordinary Christians, for that title is enough: "*agnosce, o Christiane, dignitatem tuam*: Christian, recognise your dignity".[86] And in 1969: 'There are no second-class Christians, obliged to practice only a "simplified version" of the Gospel. We have all received the same baptism, and although there is a great variety of spiritual gifts and human situations, there is only one Spirit who distributes, God's gifts, only one faith, only one hope, only one love' (cf 1 Cor 12:4-6 and 13: 1-13).[87] Both texts echo an earlier one: 'Holiness is never something second-rate, and our Lord has not called us to make the way to him easier or less heroic. He has called us to remind everyone that in any state and circumstance in life, in the midst of noble earthly involvements, they can be saints: that holiness is something accessible. And at the same time, we have to make it clear that the goal is a high one: be you perfect, as your heavenly Father is perfect (Mt 5: 48)'. For, as we read in *The Way*: 'Paradox: sanctity is more attainable than learning, but it is easier to be learned than to be a saint' (Way 282).

## Divine vocation and human vocation

One must, then, be 'faithful to one's Christian calling and to one's professional calling', the founder of Opus Dei put it on 15 August 1953: 'Our Lord has given each of us certain qualities and aptitudes, specific interests; through the various events of your life he etched your personality and you came to see a certain area of activity as the one which suited you best. Then as a result of working in that area your outlook has steadily taken a certain shape, acquiring the characteristics of that trade or profession. All this – your professional calling – you must keep, because it is something which is also part of your vocation to holiness. Our "human vocation" is a part and an important part of our "divine vocation" ' (15 October 1948).[88]

It is important to realise he is not talking of a mere juxtaposition of two loyalties – to God and to the world; no: human vocation and divine vocation are interwoven to the extent that they form one single thing in a 'unity of life'. In other words, work and all that goes with it is not just the sphere in which the ordinary Christian lives and sanctifies himself, but it is a *means* and *way* to, in fact it is the very *material* of, that sanctity.[89]

In October 1967, in a homily at Pamplona Monsignor Escrivá expressed these ideas with special vividness. He was saying Mass in the open air, before a crowd of about 40,000 people who filled one of the esplanades of the University of Navarre. He used this in fact as his point of departure: 'Reflect for a moment on the setting of our Eucharist, of our act of thanksgiving. We find ourselves in a unique temple. We might say that the nave is the university campus; the altarpiece, the university library. Over there, the machinery for constructing new buildings; above us, the sky of Navarre. . . . Surely this confirms in your minds, in a tangible and unforgettable way, the fact that everyday life is the true setting for your lives as Christians. Your ordinary contact with God takes place where your fellow men, your yearnings, your work and your affections are. There you have your daily encounter with Christ. It is in the midst of the most material things of the earth that we must sanctify ourselves, serving God and all mankind. . . . On the contrary, you must understand now more clearly that God is calling you to serve him *in and from* the ordinary, material and secular activities of human life. He waits for us every day, in the laboratory, in the operating theatre, in the army barracks, in the university chair, in the factory, in the workshop, in the fields, in the home and in all the immense panorama of work. Understand this well: there is something holy, something divine hidden in the most ordinary situations, and it is up to each one of you to discover it' (Conversations 113, 114).

'I often said to the university students and workers who were with me in the thirties that they had to know how to "materialize" their spiritual life. I wanted to keep them from the temptation, so common then and now, of living a kind of double life. On one side, an interior life, a life of relation with God: and on the other, a separate and distinct professional, social and family life, full of small earthly realities. No! We cannot lead a double life. We cannot be like schizophrenics, if we want to be Christians. There is just one life, made of flesh and spirit. And it is this life which has to become, in both soul and body, holy and filled

44

with God. We discover the invisible God in the most visible and material things. . . . Heaven and earth seem to merge, my sons and daughters, on the horizon. But where they really meet is in your hearts, when you sanctify your everyday lives'.[90]

Human vocation is not something foreign to supernatural perspectives – it is perfectly rooted in them. Divine vocation – that light by which God shows a person the root of his existence, letting him know that he expects a complete response – not only lights up his present existence but also shows up his past; this past is judged in the light of the sense of mission which faith and vocation bring with them. And all this, in the case of a Christian who realises that God wants him to be in the world, means that he realises that the whole ensemble of personal aptitudes and historical incidents which have gone to make up his human vocation are much more than just a kind of training for his divine vocation – for they form part of that vocation. In other words, one's past history and the personal situation one now finds oneself in as a result of that experience are not, for the ordinary Christian, a spring-board from which, on perceiving one's supernatural vocation, one jumps off into a different psychological and sociological world: they are something which *stays*, penetrated by a new force, it is true: but this new force does not deny or diminish them; rather it shows the deep, intimate meaning which God's will has intended them to have.

As I indicated earlier all these statements stem from a deep appreciation of the Christian dogma of creation which highlights the goodness of the world and the intimate harmony which exists in God's creating and redeeming plan: ordinary life, family affairs, everyday work, everything, vivified by grace, has a part to play in bringing to fruition the saving plans of God. 'All the things of the earth are good, not only in a natural manner but because of the supernatural order to which they have been destined' (19 March 1954). This order will be attained by man's work helped by God's grace. 'We are instruments of God co-operating with him in the true *consecratio mundi*; or, to put it more exactly, in the sanctification of the world *from within*, from the very heart of civil society' (14 February 1950). 'All the things of the earth, including material creatures, and also the earthly and temporal activities of men, have to be brought to God (and now, after sin, redeemed and reconciled), each according to its own nature, according to the immediate purpose which God has given it, but recognising its ultimate supernatural destiny in Jesus Christ: "For in him all the fullness of God was pleased to dwell, and through him to reconcile to himself all things, whether on earth or in heaven, making peace by the blood of his cross" 45

(Col 1:19-20). We have to see that Christ crowns all human activities' (19 March 1954).

One practical consequence of all this is *love for the world*. If other spiritualities, by emphasising the eschatological tension that is a feature of Christianity, led to an attitude of detachment from the world – the *contemptus mundi* – Opus Dei's spirituality, while not forgetting that tension, does emphasise that the ordinary Christian tends towards things eternal by getting involved in earthly realities. This leads to an attitude of love for the world, based on the Christian doctrine on creation and the superabundance of grace: 'We love the world because God made it good, because it came perfect from his hands and because (even if some men sometimes make it ugly and evil through sin) we have the duty to consecrate it, to return it to God: "to unite all things in him, things in heaven and things on earth" (Eph 1:10)' (19 March 1954). 'We have to love the world, work, earthly realities' (Christ passing 112). 'A man who knows that the world, and not just the temple, is the place where he finds Christ, loves that world' (Conversations 116). 'We must love the world, because it is in the world that we meet God. God shows himself, he reveals himself to us in the happenings and events of the world. Good and evil are mixed in human history, and therefore the Christian should be a man of discernment. But this discernment should never bring him to deny the goodness of God's works. On the contrary, it should bring him to recognize the hand of God working through all human actions, even those which betray our fallen nature. You could make a good motto for the Christian life out of these words of Saint Paul: "All things are yours; and you are Christ's; and Christ is God's" (1 Cor 3:22-23), and so carry out the plans of that God whose will it is to save the world'.[91]

Just a glance at these texts shows that this love of the world is a love based on Christ: it looks at the world from a supernatural point of view; the world is something that can be vivified by a Christian who realises he is inserted in Christ through faith and the sacraments.[92] It is a love which contains standards: it is aware of the fact of sin and its consequences; neither of these aspects leads to a diminution of that love; rather it is reaffirmed. For the presence of grace brings into the picture the redeeming power of a God who does not turn his back on creation but pours gifts upon it to free it from its restrictions and bring it to its full perfection; and awareness of the presence of sin is not an invitation to leave the world but to infuse it with the redeeming and saving effects of God's gifts. It is a question, in fact, of loving the world
46 and loving it *passionately*, not as something marginal to God, existing on

a purely earthly level, but loving it precisely because one loves it in God and from God's vantage point — for he is the source of all true love — and assessing it in terms of the great mission God has given it.[93]

Some paragraphs from a homily by Monsignor Escrivá on Good Friday 1960 may help us go a little further into this subject of the Christian's love for the world, his faithfulness to his human vocation. 'Being a Christian', he begins, 'is not something incidental; it is a divine reality that takes root deep in our life. It gives us a clear vision and strengthens our will to act as God wants.' Therefore, he goes on, the Christian is aware that man's pilgrimage in the world has to be completely impregnated with the spirit of Christ, as practised by a person who realises the radical nature of 'the love which Jesus Christ showed by dying for us'.

At this point he stops to describe what should be the attitude of the Christian to history, in contrast to 'the kind of attitude which develops if one is unable to penetrate the mystery of Jesus' love. Some people tend to see Christianity as a collection of devout practices, failing to realize the relation between them and the circumstances of ordinary life, including the urgency to meet the needs of other people and remedy injustice. I would say that anyone who has that attitude has not yet understood the meaning of the incarnation. The Son of God has taken the body and soul and voice of a man; he has shared our fate, even to the extent of experiencing the excruciating anguish of death. Yet perhaps without wanting to, some people regard Christ as a stranger in the world of man' (Christ passing 98).

But that is not the only kind of mistaken view: 'Others tend to imagine that in order to remain human we need to play down some central aspects of Christian dogma. They act as if the life of prayer, continual relationship with God, implied fleeing from responsibilities and forsaking the world. But they forget that it was none other than Jesus who showed us the extreme to which we should go in love and service . . . . What illuminates our conscience is faith in Christ, who has died and risen and is present in every moment of life. Faith moves us to play our full part in the changing situations and in the problems of human history. In this history, which began with the creation of the world and will reach its fulfillment at the end of time, the Christian is no expatriate. He is a citizen of the city of men, and his soul longs for God. While still on earth he has glimpses of God's love and comes to recognize it as the goal to which all men on earth are called' (Christ passing 98, 99).

It is difficult to put any more clearly this affirmation of the value of the world *and* the theological perspective from which one affirms that value. This should help us better understand the phrase we have been commenting on: 'your human vocation is a part, and a principal part, of your divine vocation'. There is an intimate harmony between both vocations precisely because the divine vocation, since it reveals the origin and ultimate end of all beings and their actions (God and his saving design), shows up the deep meaning of all reality and, therefore, of human vocation. Divine and human vocation relate to each other, in a way, as form does to matter; as something which gives meaning, and something which becomes meaningful. Therefore Monsignor Escrivá's vigorous affirmation of the world, work and history is not based on activism or on a mystique which is trapped in a purely earthly framework: it opens out onto a vivid perception of the eternal, transcendent dimensions of each and every one of our actions, even our least actions, seen as opportunities to encounter God, and as a sharing in his plan of redemption which begins in time but reaches its term in eternity.

So, the spirituality of Opus Dei is one of unity between the secular and the theological: it is a theological experience of earthly activities. 'Joining everyday work with the ascetical struggle and with contemplation (this may seem impossible but it is necessary if the world is to be reconciled with God) and turning that ordinary work into a means of personal sanctification and of apostolate: is not this a fine and noble ideal, worth giving your life for?' (19 March 1934). This is echoed in the 1950 papal decree of approval of Opus Dei: referring to the profound unity of life which the spirit of Opus Dei fosters, it affirms, using Monsignor Escrivá's own words, 'the need and, as it were, the supernatural instinct to purify all one's actions, raising them to the order of grace, to sanctify them and turn them into a means of apostolate'.[94]

## Work and work well done

In this unity of life, divine vocation, the supernatural light of faith and grace are, so to speak, the spirit, soul and source of energy; human vocation, one's personal situation in the world, is the body which this spirit gives life to. The Christian's life does not originate in himself but in God; however, this life of grace transforms his very existence deep within him. Working outwards from the very core of his free personality, it affects all aspects of his existence; *and* this happens with the person's free cooperation. From this it is easy to see the importance which work, as a basic fact of human life, has in the dynamism of the spiritual life of the ordinary Christian: if grace ought inform human life and

48  work occupies a decisive place in that life, you can immediately under-

stand that it is not the source (God and his grace are the source) but it is the axis on which sanctification operates, 'it is the hinge on which our calling to holiness is fixed and turns' (Friends 62).

These words are exactly in parallel to what he says about the harmony and interconnection between divine vocation and human vocation; they both go back to the same thing – the affirmation of the value of earthly realities not from a history-bound and social perspective but from a theological one; they stem from a faith which appreciates the divine meaning of creation. But now let us look at the idea of work as a *hinge* of sanctification. Monsignor Escrivá has summed up in a phrase all the implications of this ideal: 'you have to sanctify your work, be sanctified in your work and sanctify through your work'[95] (bearing in mind that by work he means not just work in the narrow sense but all the social interpersonal relationships which derive from it, i.e. the whole range of ordinary life insofar as it is coloured by work).[96]

Normally when Monsignor Escrivá used these words he used them in that order: i.e. he first spoke about 'sanctifying your work'. This was no accident: it ties in with his whole spiritual message: personal holiness (sanctifying yourself in your work) and apostolate (sanctifying through your work) are not two things which you attain by using your work as if it were a third element, outside holiness and outside apostolate. Rather you achieve holiness and apostolate *through* work: work is completely rooted in the dynamism of Christian living and therefore it should be sanctified in itself.[97] So let us take a closer look at the scope of this 'sanctifying work'.

First, one clarification: the Christian living in the world should elevate his human vocation into his divine vocation, and this elevation must be done without undermining the perfection which the human side of things should strive for: creatures have to be brought to God 'each according to its own nature, according to the purpose that God has given it' (19 March 1954). For lay people it is especially important not to misuse things: they should be used without ever forgetting the need to respect the particular nature of each, the authority which earthly things have in their own sphere. What is at stake is the sincerity of lay people's own lives, inserted as they are in temporal structures, and the divine mission which has linked them to those very structures. Solid competence in the human sphere, in the sphere of work, is important for the Christian from the point of view of both his loyalty to the earthly city and his loyalty to his supernatural vocation.

Living one's human vocation as part of one's divine vocation means in the first instance striving to attain real competence in the strictly 49 technical, human side of one's work. As the founder of Opus Dei put it in a homily: 'If we want to live this way, sanctifying our profession or job, we really must work well, with human and supernatural intensity' (Christ passing 50). And in *The Way* he says 'You pray, you deny yourself, you work in a thousand apostolic activities, but you don't study. You are useless then unless you change. Study – professional training of whatever type it be – is a grave obligation for us'.[98] 'What I have always taught, over the last forty years, is that a Christian should do all honest human work, be it intellectual or manual, with the greatest perfection possible: with human perfection (professional competence) and with Christian perfection (for love of God's will and as a service to mankind). Human work done in this manner, no matter how humble or insignificant it may seem, helps to shape the world in a Christian way. The world's divine dimension is made more visible and our human labour is thus incorporated into the marvellous work of creation and redemption. It is raised to the order of grace. It is sanctified and becomes God's work, *operatio Dei, opus Dei.*'[99]

There are in fact many reasons to call for this perfection:

(a) In the first place, human maturity: faithfulness to his human vocation stirs a person to work not just hard and solidly[100] but also efficiently i.e. with professional competence. 'As a motto for your work', Monsignor Escrivá commented in a homily, 'I can give you this one: *If you want to be useful, serve.* For, in the first place, in order to do things properly, you must know how to finish them properly . . . It's not enough to want to do good; we must know how to do it. And, if our desire is real, it will show itself in the effort we make to use the right methods, *finishing* things well, achieving human perfection' (Christ passing 50). 'An essential part of this task (the sanctification of ordinary work) which God has entrusted to us is the excellence of the work itself, a perfection which is also human, the proper fulfilment of all professional and social obligations. The Work requires all its members to work conscientiously, with a spirit of responsibility, with love and perseverance, without casualness or superficiality: "Do not for the sake of food destroy the work of God" Rom 14:20' (31 May 1954).

(b) But, in addition to this human authenticity, Christian faith should be a motive making for good work: we should realise that our work is being done in God's presence and in fulfilment of his command. It is no good offering to God something that is less perfect than our poor human limitations permit. The work that we offer must be without blemish and it must be done as carefully as possible, even in its smallest details, for God will not accept shoddy workmanship. "Thou shalt not offer anything that is faulty", Holy Scripture warns us, because it would not be worthy of him (Lev 22:20). For that reason, the work of each one of us, the activities that take up our time and energy, must be an offering worthy of our Creator. It must be *operatio Dei*, a work of God that is done *for* God: in short, a task that is complete and faultless'.[101] Fr Alvaro del Portillo, commenting on this aspect of Monsignor Escrivá's teaching has written:

> A person who aspires to holiness cannot be content to be mediocre. And to avoid mediocrity we have to make a constant effort in all fields using the specific means which the Work proposes to and requires of us – the sanctification of ordinary work changed into a training-ground in which our ascetical struggle is daily carried on. A work done without respite, with the desire of increasing the value of our actions day by day, following also in this the inspirations of the sanctifying Spirit who lives in us and who has wished to foster a new organised form of looking for Christian perfection precisely (and this is the great novelty) by means of the sanctification of ordinary, everyday work, each in his own state and all in the middle of the world. Therefore, our founder writes: 'Work is for us the axis around which must turn all our effort to attain Christian perfection. And, looking for Christian perfection in the middle of the world, each of you should also necessarily seek human perfection in your own professional work. Thus, we can never understand those who do not do everything possible to avoid shabby work' (25 January 1961). Clearly, people who do shabby work neither improve their human conduct nor are faithful to the continuous and specific action in us of the Holy Spirit, who wants us to be generous too in the perfection with which we try to do our human task; nor can they understand us.

(c) Human maturity and awareness of the presence of God imply a third reason for doing good work – a spirit of service. Love for God and love for people go hand in hand in a Christian life, since God loves us and shows us how to love. Working in God's presence, trying to do one's job perfectly so as to make an offering acceptable to him, requires that we work in a spirit of service and love for those around us: we have to take in and develop the social dimension which work involves. Every job, in itself, is a community event; it is something which helps improve social conditions generally; it is a source of progress and well-being[102]: and all this is reinforced and becomes more demanding when the job is inspired by charity, for charity urges one to work well, effectively and efficiently so that one can make a real social contribution. 'If a Christian does not love with deeds, he has failed as a Christian, besides failing as a person. You cannot think of others as if they were digits, or rungs on a ladder on which you can rise, or a crowd to be harangued or humiliated, praised or despised, according to circumstances. Be mindful of what others are . . . children of God, with all the dignity that marvellous title entails' (Christ passing 36).[103]

(d) But serving others does not just mean contributing to their earthly welfare; above all it means bringing them closer to God, the source of all good things. Every Christian ought, out of love for other people and in response to his own baptism, bring them to know Christ. And this also calls for perfection in work, for the ordinary Christian, who lives by his profession or trade, has to back up his words with an authority which derives from a good life in which competent work plays a big part. Thus, in a homily, after quoting Christ's words about the Christian being the light of the world (cf. Mt 5:14-16), the founder of Opus Dei pointed out that 'work, of whatever kind, becomes a lamp to enlighten your colleagues and friends. That is why I usually tell those who become members of Opus Dei, and the same applies to all of you now listening to me: "What use is it telling me that so and so is a good son of mine – a good Christian – but a bad shoemaker?" If he doesn't try to learn his trade well, or doesn't give his full attention to it, he won't be able to sanctify it or offer it to our Lord. The sanctification of ordinary work is, as it were, the hinge of true spirituality for people who, like us, have decided to come close to God while remaining fully involved in temporal affairs' (Friends 61).

These four reasons for working well indicate a number of things I should like to emphasise. In the first place, 'sanctifying your work, sanctifying yourself in your work and sanctifying through your work' are not three separate goals: they are three aspects of one and the same thing: they all go to make up Christian life in the world, in which union with God and the service of others (holiness and apostolate) both presuppose and make for a good job of work. Secondly, when speaking of perfection in work Monsignor Escrivá is not just referring to technical perfection, although that is necessary; he goes further: he wants the whole ensemble of duties and relationships which derive from work to be lifted up also, following the commandment of charity. One's everyday work, he said in 1948, 'acquires a fuller and deeper meaning, when it is directed totally to God and to the salvation of souls'.[104] 'The dignity of work is based on Love. Man's great privilege is to be able to
love and to transcend what is fleeting and ephemeral. . . . This is why

man ought not to limit himself to material production. Work is born of love; it is a manifestation of love and is directed toward love' (Christ passing 48).

'But human science and technique, our knowledge of the job, should have a feature which was basic to Saint Joseph's work and should be so for every Christian: the spirit of service, the desire to contribute to the well-being of other people. Joseph's work was not self-centred, even though his active life made him a strong and forceful personality. When he worked he was aware he was carrying out God's will; he was thinking of his people, of Jesus and Mary, and of everyone in Nazareth. . . . His skilled work was in the service of others, to brighten the lives of other families in the town; and with a smile, a friendly word, a passing quip, he would restore confidence and happiness to those in danger of losing them' (Christ passing 51).

Interpersonal relationships and the whole social dimension of our lives have therefore a place in the human and Christian perfection of work. Everyday work is a sign and consequence of solidarity among men, a sharing in the common aspiration to progress and a way to the solution of all the preoccupations and problems of society, and the Christian who lives in the middle of the world, a member of the society of God and of the society of man, must be aware of his duties towards that community to which his work unites him. Insofar as he is able, he should strive to build a more just society.

Work, taken in its integrity as a human and social task, would lose its character if it were isolated from the whole network of social relationships which it involves. A person who did his own work ever so perfectly, in an isolated pursuit of self perfection or looking no further than the needs of his own family: a person who acted like this would show he was unaware of the true Christian spirit. 'A man or a society that does not react to suffering and injustice and makes no effort to alleviate them is still distant from the love of Christ's heart. While Christians enjoy the fullest freedom in finding and applying various solutions to these problems, they should be united in having one and the same desire to serve mankind. Otherwise their Christianity will not be the word and life of Jesus; it will be a fraud, a deception of God and man' (Christ passing 167).

It is true that responsibility for solving social problems does not fall equally on all the members of a society; dedication to politics is a task which calls for a special vocation, a special aptitude for channelling people's yearnings so as to shape and orientate the world around us. But even though this is true, the 'political vocation' is only a concretization of something wider which applies to everyone – the duty to have a sense of solidarity with the rest of men whenever and wherever the opportunity arises.[105]

And so everyone can be asked: 'Love justice. Practise charity. Always defend personal freedom and the right of all men to live, to work and to be cared for in illness and old age, to set up a home and to bring children into the world and to educate those children as befits each, and to be honorably treated as men and as citizens' (15 October 1948). 'Ordinary work, in the middle of the world, puts you in contact with all the problems and preoccupations of men, since they are also your own preoccupations, your own problems: you are ordinary Christians, and citizens as others are. Your faith has to guide you when it comes to forming a judgment about contingent facts and situations. You will act with full freedom, for Catholic doctrine does not impose particular technical solutions to temporal problems – but it does ask you to be sensitive to these human problems and to have sufficient sense of responsibility to face them and to find a Christian solution to them' (15 October 1948). 'Frequently, even among Catholics who seem to be responsible and devout, one finds they make the mistake of thinking that their only obligation is to fulfil their family and religious duties, and they almost don't want to hear about civic duties. It is not a question of selfishness, it is lack of formation: no one has told them clearly that the virtue of piety (part of the cardinal virtue of justice) and one's sense of Christian solidarity also mean that we should know about and help to resolve the problems that affect the whole community' (9 January 1932).

This has to be the Christian's burning desire: 'to love God and, for the love of God, lovingly to serve everyone on earth, without distinction of language, race, nation or belief, making none of those distinctions which men more or less falsely make out to exist in society' (31 May 1943).

We should realise that we are the servants of others, that we are managers of God's good things, and that we are in need of others – to whom God has entrusted other good things: a whole series of vocations interwining, with each person being called to sanctify his own role.

This, then is the panorama of a sanctification of work which is attentive to every dimension of Christian activity – technical, social, communitary. This is not the place to examine how these general principles apply in particular cases; we should bear in mind that the Christian spirit takes over man's heart by means of personal asceticism under the influence of grace. No one acquires a disposition to serve society without making a real effort; there is always the danger (particularly as one's personality and responsibilities develop) of temptation moving in; the ideal of service can become clouded, one can begin to want power for power's sake, to use one's position for personal gain. Therefore, if this sense of service is to be maintained one must practise *'the spirit of poverty*, of true detachment from the goods of the world: and *the spirit of humility*, detachment from human glory, from power: these are the sweet fruits of the contemplative soul in everyday work' (9 January 1932). In this way it will be possible 'to do one's everyday work with the wisdom of an artist, the happiness of a poet, the self-confidence of a master and a sense of modesty more persuasive than eloquence, seeking – while one looks for Christian perfection in one's work and in one's state of life in the world – the welfare of all mankind' (9 January 1932).

## Contemplatives in the middle of the world

'Sanctifying your work' is a very big subject in itself; but we must move on – to the second motto of the triptych, 'sanctifying yourself in your work'. The first thing to be said here is that the founder of Opus Dei is not referring to 'being sanctified while you are working', but to being sanctified precisely by means of work or thanks to work; work, remember, is not just the context, it is the very medium and material of holiness. 'Sanctifying yourself in work' is not independent of 'sanctifying your work': the two are intertwined.

One thing is quite clear, even at a glance: sanctifying work, doing it with the competence which one's human and divine callings require, presupposes human perfection and brings with it a growth in that perfection. It is impossible really to do a job of work properly without practising the virtues of diligence, toughness, justice, fortitude, perseverance, prudence, affability, truthfulness. . . .

It is not surprising then that in Monsignor Escriv´a's writings we find a deep appreciation of what he usually calls human virtues, i.e. the whole assembly of qualities which go to make up a fully developed person and which equip him to face up to the responsibilities he has in society. In a vocation such as that which the spirit of Opus Dei involves, grace, the supernatural life, cannot be indifferent to human personality in all its dimensions.

'Be firm. Be virile. Be a man. And then . . . be a saint.' 'Remember that your virtue may seem to be that of a saint and yet be worth nothing 55 if it is not joined to the ordinary virtues of a Christian', we read in *The Way* (22, 409). And in a homily in 1951 he said: 'There is a certain type of secularist outlook that one comes across, and also another approach which one might call "pietistic", both of which share the view that Christians somehow are not fully and entirely human. According to the former, the demands of the Gospel are such as to stifle our human qualities; whereas for the latter, human nature is so fallen that it threatens and endangers the purity of the faith. The result, either way, is the same. They both fail to grasp the full significance of Christ's Incarnation; they do not see that 'the Word was made flesh', became man, "and dwelt amongst us" (Jn 1:14). My experience as a man, as a Christian and as a priest teaches me just the opposite. There is no human heart, no matter how deeply immersed in sin, which does not conceal, like embers among the ashes, a flicker of nobility. Whenever I have sounded out such hearts, talking to them individually with the words of Christ, they have always responded . . . human virtues constitute the foundation for the supernatural virtues'. For, upright human behaviour, under the influence of grace, prepares the way for conversion and for living a real Christian life. 'If we accept the responsibility of being children of God, we will realise that God wants us to be very human. Our heads should indeed be touching heaven, but our feet should be firmly on the ground. The price of living as Christians is not that of ceasing to be human or of abandoning the effort to acquire those virtues which some have even without knowing Christ. The price paid for each Christian is the redeeming Blood of our Lord and he, I insist, wants us to be both very human and very divine, struggling each day to imitate him who is *perfectus Deus, perfectus homo*, perfect God and perfect man' (Friends 74-75).

He spoke in similar terms in 1966: 'I shall never tire of repeating this. We must be very human, for otherwise we cannot be divine' (Christ passing 166). And in 1970' 'If we are to serve others, for Christ's sake, we need to be very human. If our life is less than human, God will not build anything on it, for he normally does not build on disorder, selfishness or emptiness'.[106]

This affirmation of the value of human virtues as an integral part of the task of personal sanctification is strictly parallel to what he says about the importance of technical, professional perfection as part of the sanctification of work. But there is more than this to the sanctifying of work and being sanctified through work: both tie in with personal encounter with God. Finishing the work of creation, bringing 56 creation to God, is a task which man has to do with the help of grace and in dialogue with the Creator.

These considerations, which are important from many points of view (for they demonstrate the difference between the Christian and the pantheistic views of the world), should be stressed here, just at this point when we are moving from 'sanctification of work' to 'sanctifying yourself in work' — moving that is from the work done to the person who does it, moving therefore into the ethical, ascetical or mystical sphere, whichever you prefer to call it. I think this step has special significance: it allows us to see up to what point the affirmation of the universal call to holiness is not just a vague aspiration, but a fully understood ideal really put into practice with all its consequences. We are, in fact, at the main crossroads for really grasping the meaning of the universal call to holiness: a failure to go deep at this point could lead one either to deny, at least in practice, this call, because one thinks that it is not in fact possible for every Christian to reach full intimacy with God; or else (and this would be more serious) to tone down the whole theological horizon of Christian existence i.e. to obscure the Christian conception of the world — leading us into an impoverished humanism.

Let's speak clearly: for too long and too insistently emphasis has been put on the difficulties which secular concerns can present to the life of prayer. Expressions such as 'the cares of life', 'the temptations of the world', have been popularised by a superficial apologia for the religious state (superficial because it failed to get to the root of the phenomenon it was investigating) and a sharp hyper-intellectual counterposing of active and contemplative life.[107]

This has given rise to a lay spirituality (if it deserves the name spirituality) based on that division: you have to sanctify yourselves, lay people were told, *in spite of* the world, *in spite of* your work. The environment in which one lives, the work which fills one's day, were seen as a situation which one cannot escape from but which is confining and inhibiting. More than this, it is a chain which prevents one from bringing his whole self to God but to which (unhappy paradox) he has to stay tied by the will of a God who has not deigned to call him to higher ways, worthier and easier ways. The ascetical and psychological consequences of this whole approach are easy to guess.[108]

No: it is necessary to state very plainly that it is not in spite of work, against work, that lay people should achieve their sanctification but precisely with and through work. Vatican II has stated this, as I pointed out earlier[109], and so did Monsignor Escrivá: 'Wherever we may be, in the middle of the noise of the street or involved in human affairs — in the factory, in the university, on the farm, at the office or at home — we 57 will find ourselves in simple filial contemplation, in a constant dialogue with God. For everything – people, things, daily tasks – offer us an opportunity and topic for continuous conversation with our Lord: just as for other souls, who have a different vocation, contemplation is made easier by their leaving the world behind – the *contemptus mundi* – and the silence of the cell or the desert. Our Lord asks us, my children, only for interior silence (quietening the selfish voice of the old man), not the silence of the world: for the world cannot and should not keep quiet on our behalf' (11 March 1940). 'We see the hand of God, not only in the wonders of nature, but also in our experience of work and effort' (Christ passing 48).

So, just as he was talking about unity between human vocation and Christian vocation, now he is talking about unity between one's working life and one's conversation with God. He is not saying that the two should live side by side: earthly occupations and theological life, work and prayer: no, they have to form a complete union so that work nourishes prayer and prayer impregnates work; so that work becomes prayer and at the same time stays as work, without losing any of its human characteristics. He has often spoken along these lines: 'An hour of study, for a modern apostle, is an hour of prayer' (Way 335). And in a homily in March 1952: 'While being fully involved in his everyday work, among other men, his equals; busy, under stress, the Christian has to be at the same time totally involved with God, for he is a child of God' (Christ passing 65). 'You should try to see that, in the middle of your ordinary occupations, your whole life is turned into continuous praise of God' (28 March 1955). Finally, in a 1967 homily: 'A Christian life should be one of constant prayer, trying to live in the presence of God from morning to night and from night to morning. A Christian can never be a lonely man, since he lives in continual contact with God, who is both near us and in heaven' (Christ passing 116).

In the teaching of the founder of Opus Dei, work and prayer become one, to such an extent that they reach that peak which is contemplative life.

Monsignor Escrivá has expressed himself very clearly and explicitly on the compatibility of contemplative life and temporal occupations: the path opened by Opus Dei is 'a way of contemplative souls in the middle of the world' (19 March 1954). Saint Paul had said: 'In him [God] we live and move and have our being' (Acts 17:18). To achieve this life in God the early monks went away from the world, retiring to the solitude of their cell. But 'we live in the street, that's where our cell is: we are contemplatives in the middle of the world' (31 May 1954).

'We have to turn work into prayer and have a contemplative soul' (15 October 1948): this is an inescapable necessity because 'if we were not truly contemplative it would be difficult to persevere in Opus Dei' (2 October 1958).[110]

The unity between the theological and secular dimensions of Christian living finds here one of its greatest expressions, as the following text, part of which I have quoted already, indicates: 'For us work, which must accompany man's life on earth, is at the same time the point at which our will meets the saving will of our heavenly Father. I tell you once again: our Lord has called on each of us to stay in his own state of life and in the practice of his profession or trade, there to sanctify ourselves in our work, sanctify that work and sanctify through it. That is why the human job that we do can rightly be considered to be *opus Dei, operatio Dei*, work of God. Our Lord puts an immense value on the work of the intelligence and hands of men, the work of his sons and daughters. Acting in this way facing God, motivated by love and by desire to be of service, with a priestly soul, all man's activity takes on a genuine supernatural meaning which keeps our life united to the source of all graces. . . . Contemplative souls in the middle of the world: this is what you must always be if you are to ensure your perseverance, your faithfulness to the calling you have received. And so at every moment of our day we will be able sincerely to say: *loquere, Domine, quia audit servus tuus* (1 Kings 3:9), speak, Lord, for your servant is listening. Wherever we may be, in the middle of the noise of the street and involved in human affairs – in the factory, in the university, on the farm, at the office or at home – we will find ourselves in simple filial conversation, in a constant dialogue with God' (11 March 1940).

A very prominent trait of Monsignor Escrivá's personality was realism. He strove to set people on fire, to make them idealistic, but he never forgot that the best desires end up nowhere unless they lead to decisions, small maybe but concrete, demanding and real. He spoke in a vibrant, even poetic, way, opening vast horizons to the eye of the soul, but at the same time showing his listener the way to reach those heights, step by step. In one of his homilies he asked: 'In recommending this unbroken union with God, am I not presenting an ideal so sublime that it is unattainable by the majority of Christians? Certainly the goal is high, but it is not unattainable. The path that leads to holiness is the path of prayer; and prayer ought to take root and grow in the soul little by little, like the tiny seed which later develops into a tree with many branches' (Friends 295).

59

The existence of God is not something immediately evident to us; we tend to get distracted and be forgetful. To grow in the faith, to make it second nature for us to be aware of the presence of God, we need to devote ourselves to him alone, to give him our full attention for a while each day — stopping everything else. 'Each day try to find a few minutes of that blessed solitude which you so much need to keep your interior life going. I understand you well when you write: "Every day I do my 'few minutes' of prayer; if it weren't for that"...', we read in some points of *The Way* (304, 106) which reflect the personal experience of the founder of Opus Dei and of millions of other souls. For this reason we find in his catechesis constant references to the liturgy[111], to vocal prayer, to meditation ... even to a full plan of life, that is to say to a set of ascetical means and devout practices which provide a sort of framework which makes it easy to remember God and converse with him.[112]

These practices of piety which he recommends are taken from the ascetical and spiritual tradition of Christians. In reviving them he gives them new accents and sets them in a secular context. In other words, he does not see them as moments when you break with what you were doing, like leaving the world in which you live to go to a higher, more divine world; rather they are more intense moments of a permanent attitude — something in full continuity with the immediate past and future, for the life of prayer belongs to the essence of Christian living. It began at the first stage of faith, when we were still inarticulate children, and it should keep growing as our faith grows.[113]

'You write: "To pray is to talk with God. But what about?" About what? About him, about yourself: joys, sorrows, successes and failures, noble ambitions, daily worries, weaknesses. And acts of thanksgiving and petitions: and love and reparation. In a word: to get to know him and to get to know yourself: "to get acquainted"' (Way 91). 'We all know', he repeated many years later, 'that prayer is to talk with God. But someone may ask, "What should I talk about?" What else could you talk about but his interests and the things that fill your day? About the birth of Jesus, his years among us, his hidden life, his preaching, his miracles, his redemptive passion and death, his resurrection. And in the presence of the Triune God.... we will speak of our everyday work, of our family, of our friendships, of our big plans and little shortcomings' (Christ passing 174).

'The theme', he added, 'of my prayer is the theme of my life.' The Christian lives by God, and he finds God and loves him in his everyday
60  life; an ordinary Christian does not pray with his back to life. On the

contrary, it happens right there, seeking to discover the true meaning of that life and to live in tune with that meaning. The time he devotes to prayer focuses on that everyday life, which he realises is something he has received from God and something directed towards God; and the dialogue begun and strengthened in prayer is extended throughout all the events of his day. 'You have told me sometimes that you are like a clock out of order, which strikes at the wrong moment: you feel cold, dry and arid at the time of your prayer; and on the other hand, when it is least to be expected, in the street, in the midst of your daily activities, in the hustle and hubbub of the city, or in the concentrated calm of your professional work, you find yourself praying. . . . At the wrong moment? Possibly; but don't waste those chimes of your clock. The Spirit breathes where he will' (Way 110). Periods of prayer, practices of piety, 'will lead you, almost without your realising it, to contemplative prayer. Your soul will pour forth more acts of love, aspirations, acts of thanksgiving, acts of atonement, spiritual communions. And this will happen while you go about your ordinary duties, when you answer the telephone, get on to a bus, open or close a door, pass in front of a church, when you begin a new task, during it and when you have finished it: you will find yourself referring everything you do to your Father God' (Friends 149).

The word 'contemplation' and the expression 'contemplative life' have been common in the vocabulary of spiritual theology for centuries. For some, they refer to an intuitive and direct knowledge of the presence of God, accompanied by ecstasy and other extraordinary phenomena; for others, they mean a deep, affective and lively sense of the presence of God, the result of the development of faith, with no extraordinary perceptions or feelings; for the former, contemplation means that the subject must adopt a passive attitude; but the latter meaning does not exclude a certain activity or training on man's part.[114] Monsignor Escrivá does not go into these distinctions, and in fact in one of his homilies, after describing the route to take in order to relate to God in the middle of the most diverse earthly occupations, he asks: 'Asceticism? Mysticism? I don't mind what you call it. Whichever it is, asceticism or mysticism, does not matter. Either way, it is a gift of God's mercy. If you try to meditate, our Lord will not deny you his assistance' (Friends 308).

But he does point out one thing very clearly: prayer should take root in the Christian's soul so as to give him such a vivid awareness of the presence of God that it quite fills him and gives meaning to all the events of his everyday life.[115]

For, we must not forget, prayer, dialogue with God, which ranges over all aspects of our life 'does not cut us off from the world we live in. It does not make us strange beings out of touch with what is going on around us' (Friends 251). On the contrary, it brings us to appreciate their value in relation to both God and men; to recognise them as proper moments for living faith, hope and charity;[116] to express in deeds the spirit of service; and when the opportunity arises to unite one's own life, in little things and big things, to Christ's Cross.[117]

About ten years after the foundation of Opus Dei Monsignor Escrivá lived for some months in Burgos. He visited the great Gothic cathedral there and took from it a comparison which he used a lot with the stu dents who were with him at the time: 'I used to enjoy climbing up the cathedral towers to get a close view of the ornamentation at the top, a veritable lacework of stone that must have been the result of very patient and laborious craftsmanship. As I chatted with the young men who accompanied me I used to point out that none of the beauty of this work could be seen from below. To give them a material lesson in what I had been previously explaining to them, I would say: "This is God's work, this is working for God! To finish your personal work per- fectly, with all the beauty and exquisite refinement of this tracery stonework." Seeing it, my companions would understand that all the work we had seen was a prayer, a loving dialogue with God' (Friends 65).

'Add a supernatural motive to your ordinary work, and you will have sanctified it' (Way 359). If someone read this out of context he might see nothing but a piece of pious advice, just an invitation to raise his heart to God, offering God the work he was doing; but in the light of what has been said we realise that this reminder is also joined to the decision to christianise this activity at its core and to do it as perfectly as possible, i.e. to sanctify it. Here is that circular movement again: becoming holy in work, union with God in work, returns us to work itself, to doing it well; the sanctification of work, seen from this angle, occurs within the process of sanctifying yourself in your work. When man affirms with his intelligence the goodness of God to be found in the world around him, and with his will strives to do his human job well, offering it and himself in it as a 'holy living sacrifice, acceptable to God' (Rom 12:1), he becomes a priest of the whole of creation, and brings the created world to God. Monsignor Escrivá sums this up by saying that 'with a truly priestly soul and a completely lay outlook, all of us, united in Christ, become that "chosen race, a royal priesthood, a

62 holy nation, God's own people, that we may declare the wonderful

deeds of him who called us out of darkness into his marvellous light" (1 Pet 2:9)' (28 March 1955).

## An awareness of being a son of God

'We've got to be convinced that God is always near us. We live as though he were far away, in the heavens high above, and we forget that he is also continually by our side. He is there like a loving Father. He loves each one of us more than all the mothers in the world can love their children – helping us, inspiring us, blessing . . . and forgiving. . . .

'We've got to be filled, to be imbued with the idea that our Father, and very much our Father, is God who is both near us and in heaven.' This point in *The Way* (267) is along the same lines, and it brings us to the core[118] of the spirituality of Opus Dei – a sense of divine filiation, awareness of being children of God.

On 19 March 1934 Monsignor Escrivá said: 'We belong to Opus Dei by divine choice – *ego elegi vos* (Jn 16:6) – in order to imitate Jesus Christ our Lord in the world, *sicut filii carissimi*, as beloved children (Eph 5:1)'. And twenty years later, on 19 March 1954: 'The basis of their spiritual life [the members of Opus Dei] is a sense of being children of God: God is my Father; he is the Author of all good; he is goodness itself'. And in a homily on Holy Thursday 1960 he put it this way: 'The God of our faith is not a distant being who contemplates indifferently the fate of men – their desires, their struggles, their sufferings. He is a Father who loves his children so much that he sends the Word, the Second Person of the most Blessed Trinity, so that by taking on the nature of man he may die to redeem us. He is the loving Father who now leads us gently to himself, through the action of the Holy Spirit who dwells in our hearts' (Christ passing 84). 'The Creator has gone overboard in love of his creatures'; all human history is governed by 'an outpouring of love from the Blessed Trinity' (Christ passing 84, 85).

The awareness of God as father, a deep understanding of what our faith tells us about God's paternal love for man, brings many consequences: it gives an intimate, confident filial tone to prayer;[119] it creates in the soul a happy, optimistic, daring attitude, which is able to take on big ventures without being put off by possible difficulties;[120] it is the basis of fraternity and of spirit of service.[121] And it also provokes an awareness of the Christian value of the world: it allows us to love the world and to move about with the joy and naturalness of someone who is at home: 'Divine filiation is a joyful truth, a consoling mystery. It    63 fills all our spiritual life. More than that: precisely because we are children of God, we can contemplate everything in love and wonder as coming from the hands of our Father, God the Creator. And so we become contemplatives in the middle of the world, loving the world' (Christ passing 65).

When the Christian speaks of divine filiation he is referring to an ontological fact – the basic fact that God, in his love for men, raises them up to himself to make them, through grace, sharers in his own nature, as Saint Peter says in his second letter (2 Pet 1:4). Monsignor Escrivá comments on this, putting it in a context of prayer: he doesn't speak about 'divine filiation' but about 'a sense of divine filiation'. And by 'sense' he means a vivid and deep awareness of the nearness of him whom we know loves us[122]; or, better, he means a capacity to notice, as it were instinctively, the presence of the loved one and to react in a way pleasing to him: this occurs when one's heart is at one with the other person.

In other words, divine filiation in the preaching of the founder of Opus Dei is regarded as something which a person should appreciate better and better until it 'eventually permeates one's entire existence' because it 'is there in every thought, every desire, every affection' (Friends 146). For it is then, and only then, that it produces all its spiritual fruits.[123] Awareness of being a son (or daughter) of God, and contemplative life, come in a way to form one single thing; or perhaps the way to say it is that awareness of being a son of God gives the contemplative life its final, definitive nuance: if contemplative life means living in God's presence, awareness of being a son of God brings us to remember that that God who is present in the world and in our own heart loves us with a father's love and wants us to treat him as a father.

So Monsignor Escrivá de Balaguer, in speaking about divine filiation, invites us to let the light of faith penetrate to the very core of reality – even the centre of ordinary life, everyday work. 'All men are children of God. But a child can look upon his father in many ways. We must try to be children who realize that the Lord, by loving us as his children, has taken us into his house, in the middle of the world, to be members of his family, so that what is his is ours, and what is ours is his' (Christ passing 64). 'When faith weakens, men tend to imagine that God is far away and hardly cares for his children. They come to regard religion as a kind of appendage, something to have recourse to when there's no other remedy; they expect, with what justification one cannot say, 

64   spectacular manifestations, unusual happenings. But when faith is really

alive in the soul, one discovers instead that to follow Christ one does not have to step aside from the ordinary pattern of everyday life and also that the great holiness which God expects of us is to be found here and now, in the little things of each day' (Friends 312).

For a Christian whose faith is alive, the things around him, the things that happen around him, are not meaningless or opaque events – veils which prevent him from seeing farther; they are calls, invitations from God, because 'our Lord is calling us constantly in a thousand little events of each day' (24 March 1930). 'There is something holy, something divine, hidden in the most ordinary situations, and it is up to each one of you to discover it' (Conversations 114). 'The Holy Spirit, living in your soul in grace – God with you – is giving a supernatural tone to all your thoughts, desires and actions (The Way 273) and so 'although we live in the world and share in all the concerns and tasks of society, our vocation is necessarily contemplative: we are in continuous, simple and filial union with God, our Father' (2 October 1958).

The contemplative life, awareness that God is our Father, fill one's horizon and create in the soul a realisation that it is worth while to give oneself completely, to launch out energetically to fulfil God's plans. 'Be a little child; the greatest daring is always that of children. Who cries for . . . the moon? Who is blind to dangers in getting what he wants? To such a child add much grace from God, the desire to do his Will, great love for Jesus, all the human knowledge he is capable of acquiring, and you will have a likeness of the apostles of today such as God undoubtedly wants them' (Way 857).

This daring, this confidence deriving from awareness of the fatherly nearness of God, may in certain circumstances impel a person to exceptional, extraordinary actions.[124] But its effectiveness is not confined to cases like that. In fact, if someone got only that far, he would still not have grasped key aspects of the Christian faith: he would fail to see that this faith invites him to see God also in ordinary life, in even the unimportant events of daily work, in simple natural family life and relations with friends and colleagues – in the little things of everyday life.

It is good to read the whole chapter in *The Way* on this subject – the chapter on 'Little Things': there you will see the key position Monsignor Escrivá gives them in Christian and specifically in lay spirituality.[125] They are in fact a sure way for ordinary Christians to reach God: 'You have mistaken the way if you despise the little things.' 'Do you really want to be a saint? Carry out the little duty of each moment: do what you ought and concentrate on what you are doing' 65

(Way 816, 815). 'Someone may imagine that there is little in ordinary life that can be offered to God: insignificant little things, nothing really. A little child who wants to please his father offers him what he has: a headless toy soldier, an empty spool, a few coloured stones, two buttons — everything 'valuable' he has in his pockets, his 'treasures'. But his father doesn't look at the childishness of the gift: he is pleased and he hugs his son with immense tenderness. Let us behave in this way with God and then these childish things — these insignificant little things — become 'big things', for our love is big: that's our style — out of Love to make the little things of each day, each moment, something heroic'.[126]

If we examine those passages where Monsignor Escrivá speaks of 'little things', we will notice that sometimes he does so to show that the ordinary Christian is called to sanctify himself in everyday life, or to counter the tendency to escape from reality by living in a daydream. But at other times the phrase has an additional meaning: it reminds us that we have to respond to God's unceasing love for us, that we mustn't express this love only at special moments, but we should try to do it all the time, in all the events of our day.

He wants us to have a lively faith which leads us to discover God in everyone and in every event — and on this basis to have a lively charity which influences our every action, no matter how small, even though humanly speaking it may seem insignificant or even contemptible. Looked at with the eyes of faith even these small things are found to be full of meaning, capable of incarnating the love of God: 'Do everything for love. Thus there will be no little things: everything will be big'.[127]

In this way every Christian life is a calling to go the whole way. A person who is faithful to grace can live like this, in some way tasting what Saint Paul described: 'God begins to be all in all' (cf. 1 Cor 15:28). And from this vantage point we can see that all human activities, other than those stained by sin, are valuable; they are in fact important, decisive, crucial, insofar as they mark the place where we meet God and the time when we show our love by giving ourselves to him and to the service of our fellows. 'It is time for us Christians to shout from the rooftops that work is a gift from God and that it makes no sense to classify men differently, according to their occupation, as if some jobs were nobler than others. Work, all work, bears witness to the dignity of man, to his dominion over creation' (Christ passing 47).

'Christ wishes to become incarnate in our things, to vivify from within even our most insignificant actions. . . . This thought is a clear, objective, supernatural reality. It is not a pious consideration to comfort those of us who will never get our names inscribed in the annals of history. Christ is interested in the work we do — whether once or thousands of times — in the office, in the factory, in the shop, in the classroom, in the fields, in the exercise of any manual or intellectual occupation' (Christ passing 174).[128] For the history of our lives is a history whose consequences are not confined to this earth: it is a history which is called to flow into the fulness of the kingdom of heaven.

It should be obvious that when we speak of the sense of divine filiation and of the value of little things we are speaking of joy, confidence, serenity, interior peace — and also demands. Monsignor Escrivá is not imagining a superficial, simplistic, dreamy panorama for the ordinary Christian: he is asking for a serious commitment; for an attitude, not of mediocrity, but of heroism; for vitality not casualness, because 'perseverance in little things for Love is heroism' (Way 813). A love which goes into detail can only be lived by a constantly renewed decision. 'In your interior life, have you slowly considered the beauty of "serving" with ever-renewed willingness?' (Way 293). and elsewhere he reminds us that 'Jesus isn't satisfied "going halves": he wants everything (Way 155); 'What is the secret of perseverance? Love. Fall in love and you will not leave him' (Way 999). From this he goes on to conclude: 'Jesus, may I be the last in everything . . . and first in Love' (Way 430). A living faith, a constant exercise of free will, and love are the pillars of the interior attitude which allows a Christian living in the world to find God in the daily events and duties which go to make up his life of work and in this way endow the ordinary with a divine, absolute and infinite value.

## Work and apostolate

Sanctifying ordinary work, trying to do a job which is humanly perfect and is full of divine energy; being sanctified by work, making use of work to live a contemplative life: the two first points in Monsignor Escrivá's motto. Now we will look at the third dictum: 'sanctifying through your work'.

The search for holiness has sometimes been presented as an absorbing activity which gets in the way of other occupations and so takes one away from other people. But that is a caricature of Christianity. Charity, the love which is born of Christian faith, is indivisible: loving God, being identified with him, consists in sharing the love with which God loves, being 'divinised' with a divinisation which by 'bringing you 67 nearer your Father, will make you more of a brother to your brother men' (Way 283). The search for personal holiness and a spirit of service to others are two sides of the same coin, two simultaneous and inseparable attitudes.

Monsignor Escrivá defended this doctrine throughout his life and rejected any language which separated holiness from apostolate, the search for God from the service of others. He realised that any attempt to isolate or oppose these two activities stemmed either from a false interior life i.e. unauthentic, purely verbal piety, usually a cover for selfishness; or else from a naturalistic approach which understands the service of others in a purely earthly sense — excluding therefore the more radical and definitive form of service which is telling people about God. If the former causes a person to turn in on himself in a selfish, individualistic way, the latter leads him to underrate interior life, to impoverish the human dimension of things and deprive man of the only Good of which he is absolutely in need; in both cases the Christian spirit is either paralysed or destroyed.

Every Christian should regard as addressed to himself Jesus' words when he sent out the Apostles — the words which made them apostles, men sent out: '"Go, preach the Gospel. . . . I will be with you. . . " It is Jesus who has said this . . . and he has said it to you' (Way 904). Monsignor Escrivá comments (6 March 1945): 'You cannot separate the fact that Christ is God-Man from his role as redeemer. The Word became flesh to save men, to make them one with him: that is why he came to the world. We are other Christs, called to co-redeem, and therefore we cannot section off our life as sons of God, in his Work, separating it from our apostolic zeal'.[129]

'An apostle — that is what a Christian is, when he knows that he has been grafted onto Christ, made one with Christ, in baptism. He has been given the capacity to carry on the battle in Christ's name, through confirmation. He has been called to serve God by his activity in the world, because of the common priesthood of the faithful, which . . . gives him the capacity to take part in the worship of the Church and to help other men in their journey to God, with the witness of his word and his example, through his prayer and work of atonement'.[130]

This orientation towards apostolate, which is a feature of every Christian vocation, takes on a particular tonality in the case of lay people. The Christian who lives in the middle of the world in daily contact with others, with their joys, their interests, their yearnings and their desire — hidden perhaps, but still there — for union with God, should give expression to the faith which is the life of his soul: 'If we have this desire for contemplation in the middle of the world – in the street, in the open air, under the sun, in the rain – not only will we want to remain at our temporal task, so as not to cut ourselves off from earthly realities, but we will also be impelled by an apostolic desire bravely to penetrate all these secular structures, to discover the divine demands they contain, to show that the brotherhood of the children of God – human fraternity has a supernatural meaning – is the great solution offered for the problems of the world: to release men from their shell of selfishness: at the same time to guarantee, to those immersed in the mass of society, their rightful personality and true freedom – 'when Christ freed us, he meant us to remain free (Gal. 5:1): in a word, to open up for men the divine paths of the earth' (11 March 1940).

'The apostolic concern which burns in the heart of ordinary Christians is not something separate from their everyday work. It is part and parcel of one's work, which becomes a source of opportunities for meeting Christ. As we work at our job, side by side with our colleagues, friends and relatives and sharing their interests, we can help them come closer to Christ' (Friends 264). The Christian's secular and work situation does not in anyway change when he realises the apostolic dimension of his divine vocation: 'What has changed? There is a change inside our soul, now that Christ has come aboard, as he went aboard Peter's boat. Its horizon has opened wider. It feels a greater ambition to serve and an irrepressible desire to tell all creation about the *magnalia Dei* (Act 2:11), the marvellous things our Lord does, if only we let him act in us.'[131]

But how are work and apostolate combined in practice? We should bear in mind that the word 'apostolate' refers to a whole range of things from the actual verbal announcing of Christ to people's efforts to infuse a Christian spirit into environments and institutions. Apostolate is, Vatican II states, all activity aimed at 'spreading the kingdom of Christ everywhere for the glory of God the Father, so that all may share in Christ's saving redemption and so that through them the whole world may be in fact brought into relationship with him'[132] In Monsignor Escrivá's writings it has this broad meaning; for example: 'Lay people have their own way of contributing to the holiness and apostolate of the Church. They do so by their free and responsible action within the temporal sphere, to which they bring the leaven of Christianity. Giving Christian witness in their everyday lives, spreading the word which enlightens in the name of God, acting responsibly in the service of others and thus contributing to the solution of common problems: these are some of the ways in which ordinary Christians fulfil their 69 divine mission' (Conversations 59).

Leaving to one side for a moment the third of these ways (activity aimed at directing the world towards God) let us consider the other two — word and witness — to see how Monsignor Escrivá links them to work.

(a) *Apostolate and the Christian word*: 'All the circumstances in which life places us bring a divine message, asking us to respond with love and service to others . . . . We must learn to recognise Christ when he comes out to meet us in our brothers, the people around us. No human life is ever isolated. It is bound up with other lives. No man or woman is a single verse; we all make up one divine poem which God writes with the cooperation of our freedom' (Christ passing 111). We are born and we live among men — and this involves us in relationships and friendships. Our Christian faith, lighting these up from the inside, endows them with a deeper meaning. And so, apostolate arises, as a prolongation of friendship and family and social links: 'We must translate into deeds and truth the great desire of God "who wishes all men to be saved and to come to the knowledge of the truth" ( 1 Tim 2:4) (Friends 230); apostolate is giving ourselves to others, to reveal Christ to them and lead them to God the Father' (Christ passing 49).

In the case of an ordinary Christian, speaking about God, making known the divine meaning of everyday life, spreading to others the faith he has received: all this is interwoven with work, the events that frame it, the conversations it gives rise to: it is not just that apostolate happens in the work situation: it is based on work and on the whole tissue of family and social relations. 'My joy is your joy, because you remain secure in the certainty that through the vocation we have received our *ordinary work* in the world — each person's own job — is our most effective specific means for attaining Christian perfection doing a fruitful apostolate' (15 October 1948). 'For since we live in the same circumstances as others, sharing all their preoccupations and problems, we try to live and work with them with such charity that they be drawn closer to God. We let everyone see that work, however humble it be, is an exalting thing if it is well done for a supernatural motive. Even more: this spiritualisation of human tasks allows us to co-operate through our work in the divine work of Redemption and to feel truly brothers of the great family of the sons and daughters of God' (14 February 1950).

The result is that this showing forth of God and bringing people to him, the nucleus of apostolic endeavour, is expressed in simple, natural, and ordinary words. The ordinary member of the faithful does not operate by virtue of a mandate from church authority; his only claim of right to do apostolate – and it is perfectly adequate – is his status as a Christian. The word he speaks goes from friend to friend, from colleague to colleague, in an apostolate which happens when you 'travel together the way of professional and civic life' (15 August 1953) – an apostolate which the founder of Opus Dei has called one of 'friendship and trust': 'those well-timed words, whispered into the ear of your wavering friend; the helpful conversation you managed to start at the right moment; the ready professional advice that improves his university work; the discreet indiscretion by which you open up unexpected horizons for his zeal. This all forms part of the "apostolate of friendship"' (Way 973).

In a homily in 1954, after recalling that every Christian has received the mission of making Christ known, he explains himself more fully: 'Perhaps someone will ask how we are to bring this knowledge of Christ to others. And I reply: naturally, simply, living as you live in the middle of the world, devoted to your professional work and to the care of your family, sharing the noble interests of men, respecting the rightful freedom of every person. . . .

'If we act in this way, we give those around us the example of a simple and normal life which is consistent, even though it has all the limitations and defects which are part and parcel of the human condition. And when they see that we live the same life as they do, they will ask us: Why are you so happy? How do you manage to overcome selfishness and comfort-seeking? Who has taught you to understand others, to live well and to spend yourself in the service of others? Then we must disclose to them the divine secret of Christian existence. We must speak to them about God, Christ, the Holy Spirit, Mary. The time has come for us to use our poor words to communicate the depth of God's love which grace has poured into our souls. . . . The Christian apostolate – and I'm talking about an ordinary Christian living as just one more man or woman among equals – is a great work of teaching. Through real, personal, loyal friendship, you create in others a hunger for God and you help them to discover new horizons – naturally, simply. With the example of your faith lived to the full, with a loving word which is full of the force of divine truth' (Christ passing 148, 149).[133]

This quotation shows very clearly the core and the nature of the apostolate of friendship and trust which grows up out of work itself, out of the events of ordinary life. It is a faithful echo of the way the first Christians lived and of those well-known words of Saint Peter: 'Glorify God in your hearts and always have your answer ready for those who ask you the reason for the hope that is in you' (1 Pet 3:15).

(b) *Apostolate and witness*: 'We are not doing *our* apostolate. If we were, what could we possibly say? We are doing Christ's apostolate, because God wants it to be done and because he has commanded us to do it: "Go out all over the world, and preach the Gospel to the whole of creation" (Mk 16:15). . . . How are we to carry out this apostolate? First of all, by our example, by living according to the Will of the Father, as Jesus, with his life and teaching, taught us to do' (Friends 267-268). This is another central teaching of the founder of Opus Dei. The 1950 decree of approval already quoted, when speaking of apostolate, points out in fact that the members of Opus Dei do apostolate 'by means of the example they give to their working companions in family, civil and professional life, trying always and everywhere to be the best'.[134]

In *The Way* we read: ' "Did our hearts not burn within us as he talked to us on the road?" If you are an apostle, these words of the disciples of Emmaus should rise spontaneously to the lips of your professional companions when they meet you along the ways of their lives' (Way 917).

And in a later homily with the interesting title of 'Christ's presence among Christians', after pointing out the variety of vocations in the Church, he refers to those whom God wants 'to stay right where they are, in all the earthly occupations in which they work', and comments that these Christians should bring Christ to all the spheres in which they are acting: 'the factory, the laboratory, the farm, the trades, the streets of the big cities and the trails of the mountains. . . . Every Christian should make Christ present among men. He ought to act in such a way that those who know him sense "the fragrance of Christ" (2 Cor 2:15). Men should be able to recognize the Master in his disciples'.[135]

The four texts I have quoted indicate the importance that example and witness have in apostolate as understood by the founder of Opus Dei. At this point I should like to show the central place which work has in this witness — something we can understand only if we take work in its fullest sense i.e. along with the various relationships and duties which derive from it (identifying it therefore with the full range of ordinary life) and also in terms of doing a specific job — for one's job is what defines the ordinary Christian and if it is not done with real competence it is hollow and false. 'You stray from your apostolic way if you use the opportunity — or the excuse — offered by a work of zeal to leave the duties of your position unfulfilled. For you will lose that professional prestige which is your "bait" as a "fisher of men".'[136]

'We must avoid the error of thinking we can reduce apostolate to the performance of a few pious practices. You and I are Christians but at the same time, and without any break in continuity, we are citizens and workers, with clear obligations which we have to fulfil in an exemplary manner if we really want to become saints. Jesus himself is urging us: "You are the light of the world. A city set on a mountain cannot be hidden. Neither do men light a lamp and put it under a measure, but upon the lampstand, so as to give light to all in the house. Even so, let your light shine before men, in order that they may see your good works and give glory to your Father in heaven" (Mt 5:14-16). Professional work, whatever it is, becomes a lamp to enlighten your colleagues and friends' (Friends 61).

These and other passages reflect the effort the founder of Opus Dei had to make, especially in the early years of his work as a priest, to expand the contemporary attitude to and practice of the lay apostolate: for people saw apostolate in terms of charitable and welfare activities, Catholic apologetics, etc. – something done quite independently of the secular work of the individual Christian.[137] The point Monsignor Escrivá kept making was that apostolate is not marginal to ordinary everyday life – it is central to it. He said this because he realised that faith and charity were capable of unifying a person's whole life: this was a major feature of his thought.

Everything has its beginning, he tells us, in the centre of our soul, once the Christian realises the richness, depth, beauty – and demands – of God's love. 'Your apostolate must be the overflow of your life "within"' (Way 961). From this interior life, this relationship with God, is born the desire to speak about God and make him known – and, with it, the call to back up faith with deeds; the decision to do God's will; the effort to overcome our defects; the decision to love in spite of personal weakness; perseverance; beginning again after any falls; joy. And all this – for the Christian lives among men – is example, witness: a witness which is not sought and sometimes isn't even wanted; but it is inseparable from life; an example of work well done, of fulfilment of the duties of one's state in life, of sincere friendship, of social sensitivity, of practice of human and divine virtues; an example which has a secular and lay stamp, unostentatious, being just one citizen more; without anything usual or any pretensions to be regarded as better than others; working sincerely and simply, aware of one's own defects and trying to overcome them, – an unspectacular example, with the naturalness typical of a daily event, but real and genuine. And then the circle is closed, because this simple example, which stems from ordinary life, 73 provokes conversation with others, a dialogue about the meaning of life: apostolate in the form of the word which makes Christ known.

Between word and example there are very close links: in fact the two are inseparable in the case of lay apostolate. Words, such as the Gospel's good news, which invite a profound change in the depths of one's being, are so much more powerful when backed up by the example and personal commitment of the speaker. This point has an extra relevance in the case of the ordinary Christian who, as we have seen, acts without official mandate, representing no one, with no authority other than that which his own life gives him. Therefore, in the lay person's case, work presupposes example; example is essential. Monsignor Escrivá said this often, pointing out that this is what Christ himself did. Charity, he explained, stirs the Christian to practise all virtues – justice, solidarity, joy, friendship, etc. – for otherwise you cannot love with deeds. 'You can see immediately that the practice of these virtues leads to apostolate. In fact it already is apostolate. For when people try to live in this way in the middle of their daily work, their Christian behaviour becomes good example, witness, something which is a real and effective help to others. They learn to follow in the footsteps of Christ who "began to do and to teach", joining example with word' (Act 1:1).[138] First, action, then teaching. That was the way Christ operated: before speaking to us of love, he loved us by deed – becoming man, working for years in Nazareth, surrendering himself totally. And that is how the Christian should act too, practising love and showing love through deeds; only then will his word be fruitful.

But if word, to be fully effective, presupposes example, example in turn is directed towards word – for the root of the Christian's life goes way beyond the Christian himself and anything his deeds may say. This root is the infinite love of God, and that love can be revealed only by our word – insofar as it is an echo of the word pronounced by God himself. Therefore Monsignor Escrivá, underlining the central place example has in apostolate in the world, has also insisted that it must not be a mute example: it must be open to being articulated, it must be directed towards speech. 'Filling the world with light, being salt and light: that was how our Lord described the mission of his disciples. To bring to the ends of the earth the good news of God's love. All of us Christians should devote our lives to doing this, in one way or another. . . . Each of us has to be not only an apostle, but an apostle of apostles, bringing others along, so that they in turn will encourage others to make Jesus Christ known to everyone' (Christ passing 147).

74 'If you were to fall into the temptation of wondering, "Who's telling

me to embark on this?" we would have to reply: "Christ himself is telling you, is begging you." The harvest is plentiful enough, but the labourers are few. You must ask the Lord to whom the harvest belongs to send labourers out for the harvesting" (Mt 9: 37-38). Don't take the easy way out. Don't say, "I'm no good at this sort of thing; there are others who can do it; it isn't my line". No: for this sort of thing, there is no one else: if you could get away with that argument, so could everyone else. Christ's plea is addressed to each and every Christian. . . . Either we carry out a fruitful apostolate, or our faith will prove barren.

'Besides, who ever said that to speak about Christ and to spread his doctrine you need to do anything unusual or remarkable? Just live your ordinary life; work at your job trying to fulfil the duties of your state in life, doing your job, your everyday work, properly, improving, getting better each day. Be loyal; be understanding with others and demanding on yourself. Be mortified and cheerful. This will be your apostolate. Then, though you won't see why, because you're very aware of your own wretchedness, you will find that people come to you. Then you can talk to them, quite simply and naturally – on your way home from work for instance, or in a family gathering, on a bus, walking down the street, anywhere. You will chat about the sort of longings that everyone feels deep down in his soul, even though some people may not want to pay attention to them: they will come to understand them better, when they begin to look for God in earnest' (Friends 272-273).

In this way, through the consistency of his life and using natural simple words, arising out of the context of his work, and in the midst of it, the Christian will be leaven which ferments all the dough;[139] he will be a burning coal which warms the ways of the earth with the divine fire he bears in his heart:[140] he will be the stone fallen into the lake, which causes one circle and it another and another . . . ,[141] bringing Christ's name to the ends of the earth. And this not as the result of attitudes merely tagged on but as a result of the development of faith, hope and charity to the point where they influence one's whole everyday life. 'For a Christian apostolate is something instinctive. It is not something added onto his daily activities and his everyday work from the outside. I have repeated it constantly, since the day that our Lord chose for the foundation of Opus Dei! We have to sanctify our ordinary work, we have to sanctify others through the exercise of the particular profession that is proper to each of us, in our own particular state in life' (Christ passing 122).

Therefore the founder of Opus Dei doesn't speak so much of *doing*   75 *apostolate* as of *being apostles*. For he is not talking about spending a few hours at apostolate as if this were a marginal activity; nor of doing apostolate in the way that someone fulfils a job; but something completely different: it is a matter of sanctifying others by means of one's job, of doing one's job, *by divine vocation*, seeing it as an instrument of apostolate and as a continuous opportunity for supernatural zeal. For the lay person as I have been describing him, apostolate is not a function but rather an intention which permeates all his or her life — with a *permanent personal dedication*, which calls for no external signs. Just as charity in the movement towards God turns work into contemplative life, in the movement towards men it turns the same work into apostolic life.

Perhaps the best way to finish these lines is to quote a paragraph which illustrates the special characteristic of the approach: 'unity of life'. 'The double aspect of our aim (ascetic and apostolic) is so intrinsically and harmoniously united and bound up with the secular character of Opus Dei that it gives rise to a unity of life which is simple and strong (unity of ascetical, apostolic and professional life) and turns our whole existence into prayer, sacrifice and service in a filial relationship with the most holy Trinity: with the Father, with the Holy Spirit, with Jesus Christ, *perfectus Deus, perfectus Homo*' (14 February 1950).

## Sowers of peace and joy

The Vatican II decree on the lay apostolate states that apostolate is all activity which brings men to share in Christ's saving redemption and through them actually brings the world into relationship with him.[142] And the pastoral constitution *Gaudium et spes*, when it deals with man's activity in the world, i.e. work, reminds us that 'appointed Lord by his resurrection and given plenary power in heaven and on earth (Act 2:36: Mt 18:18), Christ is now at work in the hearts of men through the energy of his Spirit. He arouses not only a desire for the age to come, but by that very fact, he animates, purifies, and strengthens those noble longings too by which the human family strives to make its life more human and to render the whole earth submissive to this goal. . . . Therefore, while we are warned that it profits a man nothing if he gain the whole world and lose himself (cf Lk 9:25), the expectation of a new earth must not weaken but rather stimulate our concern for cultivating this one. For here grows the body of a new human family, a body which even now is able to give some kind of foreshadowing of the new age.'[143]

In the writings of Monsignor Escrivá we find many very valuable insights, often connected with a text from Saint John's Gospel which, from 7 August 1931, he kept very close to his heart: 'And when I am lifted up from the earth, I shall draw all things to myself' (Jn 12:32). 'For many years now, ever since the foundation of Opus Dei, I have meditated and asked others to meditate on those words of Christ which we find in Saint John: "And when I am lifted up from the earth, I shall draw all things to myself" (Jn 12:32). By his death on the Cross, Christ has drawn all creation to himself. Now it is the task of Christians, in his name, to reconcile all things with God, placing Christ, by means of their work in the middle of the world, at the summit of all human activities' (Conversations 59). 'Christ our Lord was crucified: from the height of the cross he redeemed the world, thereby restoring peace between God and men. Jesus reminds all of us: "And I, if I be lifted up from the earth, I will draw all things to myself" (Jn 12:32). If you put me at the centre of all earthly activities, he is saying, by fulfilling the duty of each moment, in what appears important and what appears unimportant, I will draw everything to myself. My kingdom among you will be a reality!'[144]

Many of the teachings discussed in recent pages hinge on what is said in these texts. Let me take two in particular: first, the deep grasp of the identification of the Christian with Christ or, if you like, the deep awareness of the presence of Christ in the Christian with the purpose of continuing his work of redemption; and secondly, the view of salvation history as the effect of God the Father's paternal love: he made the world good and when it was damaged by sin he did not leave it but sent his only-begotten Son to raise up on earth 'a new race of the sons of God', whose role would be to re-establish the harmony of creation. God's call puts before man a goal which transcends history, and grace will not produce all its fruits until after death; but God, by way of pledge and earnest, has already granted us his gifts and this divinization of our personality reverberates over all creation: the Christian, *alter Christus, ipse Christus*, another Christ, Christ himself, is already drawing all things towards God.

Nothing could be further from Monsignor Escrivá's thought than any reductionist approach which would turn the Gospel into an earth-bound message. His rich humanity, which made him feel deep yearnings which only God could satisfy, and, particularly, his faith and his constant wonder at the goodness of God who not only created men but raises them to the status of his children: all this made him react strongly against reductionism; it 'belittled the faith'.[145] 'Christian apostolate is not a political programme or a cultural alternative. It implies the spreading of good, "infecting" others with a desire to love, sowing peace and joy.'[146] The word of the Gospel is addressed to man's heart in order to show him God's love, which is the great truth, transcending all temporal achievements. The Christian, looking at life, should see that 'life on earth, which we love, is not definitive. "We do not have a permanent dwelling-place here, but we seek that which is to come" (Heb 13:14), a changeless home' (Christ passing 126).

But this awareness of being wayfarers should not turn the Christian into a 'defeatist with regard to human nature' (Christ passing 125). 'Still, we must be careful not to interpret the Word of God within limits that are too narrow. Our Lord does not expect us to be unhappy in our life on earth and await a reward only in the next life. God wants us to be happy on earth too, but with a desire for the other, total happiness that only he can give.

In this life, the contemplation of supernatural reality, the action of grace in our souls, our love for our neighbour as a result of our love for God: all these are already a foretaste of heaven, a beginning that is destined to grow from day to day. We Christians cannot resign ourselves to leading a double life: our life must be a strong and simple unity into which all our actions converge' (Christ passing 126).

This gives rise to an attitude which combines a life of prayer, appreciation for the gifts God has given us, human joy, a yearning for eternity, work, an effort to express love of God in the world, a sense of friendship, a desire to help others, 'making lovable their way of holiness in this world'.[147] And all this is built around awareness of divine filiation and a desire to have 'Christ crown all human activities'. For, the phrase 'when I am lifted up from the earth' is seen by Monsignor Escrivá as both a proclamation and a commandment: a proclamation of Christ's triumph and a commandment from Christ to Christians for them to make him present in the very centre of the world, not through mere external signs,[148] but in a much more radical way: they personally must be Christ: they must allow the Holy Spirit to go deep into their souls, to fill them with a new life, the life of Christ which, by expressing itself in deeds, spreads the effects of grace throughout the world. It is a matter, then, of sanctifying human activities – but not in an extrinsic or artificial way: rather, *from within*: they personally have to be Christian and then they will spontaneously transmit to their own actions their own lifeblood.[149]

To understand how Monsignor Escrivá approaches the question of
78  the effects of this impact of the kingdom of Christ on the world we

must first look at a key question – his teaching on the subject of freedom, or rather his love for freedom[150]. He spoke of freedom at two
levels, one theological, the other social and ecclesiological; both of
them very important.

(a) Monsignor Escrivá considered freedom above all as a basic com-
ponent of salvation history: God, who loves men not as slaves but as
friends and children, seeks not forced responses but free decisions. 'By
creating us God has run the risk and engaged in the adventure of our freedom. He wants human history to be something genuine, something made
up of genuine decisions – not something fictitious or a game.'[151] 'I
readily understand those words of Saint Augustine, Bishop of Hippo,
which ring out like a wonderful hymn to freedom, "God who created
you without you, will not save you without you"'.[152] 'This hymn to
freedom is echoed in all the mysteries of our Catholic faith' (Friends
25). 'When God our Lord gives us his grace, when he calls us by a
specific vocation, it is as if he were stretching out his hand to us, in a
fatherly way. A strong hand, full of love, because he seeks us out individually as his own sons and daughters, knowing our weakness. The
Lord expects us to make the effort to take his hand, his helping hand.
He asks us to make an effort and show we are free' (Christ passing 17).
Freedom is here shown to us as something based on God; it is grasped
in all its fullness and the same time it is understood as an energy which
is not locked within itself but, rather, reaches its full expression in self
surrender, in love. Freedom locates man at a crossroads: he must
choose love or selfishness, fullness or fall; and this gives history the
character of a drama which is for real and which therefore man must
approach responsibly.[153]

(b) This appreciation of the value of freedom – which derives from
the very core of the Gospel – leads one to love freedom not only in itself but in people as well. This brings us to the 'sociological' level of
freedom. Into this tie other basic convictions of Monsignor Escrivá: his
conviction that all temporal occupations have to be sanctified from
within, respecting their nature, without instrumentalising them or
manipulating them; his acute perception of the transcendence of faith:
faith cannot be reduced to mere ideology; his clear awareness of the
limits of every human mind: this gives one a critical attitude towards
one's own personal views and disposes one to dialogue. . . .

Let us stay for a moment on that last point: 'If my own personal
experience is of any help, I can say that I have always seen my work as
a priest and shepherd of souls as being aimed at helping each person to
face up to all the demands of his life and to discover what God wants 79

from him in particular – without in any way limiting that holy independence and blessed personal responsibility which are the features of a Christian conscience. This way of acting and this spirit are based on respect for the transcendence of revealed truth and on love for the freedom of the human person. I might add that they are also based on a realization that history is undetermined and open to a variety of human options – all of which God respects' (Christ passing 99).

Faith enlightens the Christian about the ultimate meaning of life and events, but it does not give him the key to understanding everything that happens: this is left 'for men to work out. Let us not forget that God, who gives us the sure ground of faith, has not revealed to us the meaning of all human events. Alongside things which to the Christian are certain and sure, there are very many others about which we can have only opinions: that is to say, a kind of knowledge which may be true and reasonable but which we cannot state incontrovertibly. For not only is it possible that I may be wrong but it is also possible that I may be right and others may also be right. Something which I see as concave will look convex to people who are seeing it from a different position'.[154]

A little earlier, in the same article, he had said: 'There are no dogmas on temporal matters. It is not in keeping with man's dignity to try to lay down absolute truths in questions which each person necessarily has to look at from his own point of view, according to his own interests, his cultural preferences and his own particular experience. Any attempt to impose dogmas in temporal matters leads, inevitably, to abusing other peoples' consciences, to not respecting one's neighbour'.[155]. By this I don't mean that the position a Christian taken up in temporal questions should be one of indifference or apathy. But I do think that a Christian has to combine his human passion for civic and social progress with an awareness of the limitations of his own opinions: so he has to respect other peoples' opinions and love legitimate pluralism. If a person did not live like that, he would not really have grasped the Christian message'.[156]

Moving away from the subject of freedom let us go back to the question of the impact of faith on social and cultural life.

In the first place, I should point out that Monsignor Escrivá de Balaguer never set out exhaustively to examine the effects which this faith could produce (he didn't like the theoretical approach); but in his writings he does mention many things which could and ought to be considered as temporal effects of the action of grace: social improvement, technical progress and cultural development, which influence man's effort to produce good work, work which is technically competent; a responsible approach to one's duties and obligations, and sensitivity to evil and injustice, which derive from the Christian precept of charity, etc., etc. Should I be content with a mere list or should I try to place these in order? I think I ought try to do the latter because familiarity with his writings does show that he puts a main emphasis on charity, which moves one to love others and, along with or, better, within this, the values of living in harmony with other people of like or different views. One might be inclined to ask: Would it not be more logical, considering that work is the hinge of his spirituality, to put the accent on technical efficiency, on dominion over, and exploration of, nature and that sort of thing? But you are no longer surprised when you look at it more carefully and you remember the very broad concept he has of work — not just busying your hands, but a real commitment which roots a person in community life — and you realise the importance he gives to freedom and therefore his view of history as an expression of the love to which freedom is directed. Material achievements and technical efficiency are never forgotten — in fact they are presupposed and explicitly affirmed, but within a much fuller vision of man.

Society, it is true, requires economic goods, organisational structures, etc., etc.; but as a specifically human reality society has to do primarily with sharing, dialogue, cooperation, friendships. And it is at this level precisely that the Christian spirit introduces an essential light. No one is genuinely Christian unless he loves with the same full heart as Christ loves with, unless he realises he is the bearer of a word which must reach to the very ends of the earth, overcoming all barriers and divisions. Christianity impells us to 'behave as God's children towards all God's children' (Christ passing 36), to practise a 'spirit of charity, of harmony, of understanding' (Conversations 35); to root out of our lives 'everything which is an obstacle to Christ's life in us — attachment to our own comfort, the temptation to selfishness, the tendency to be the centre of everything' (Christ passing 158); to destroy those idols which make people totally selfish or turn them into slaves — 'the idols of misunderstanding, of injustice, of ignorance, and of those who claim to be self-sufficient and arrogantly turn their backs on God' (Friends 105); 'to show the charity of Christ and its concrete expression in friendship, understanding, human affection and peace' (Christ passing 166).

Christians ought to be, in the world, 'sowers of peace and joy'.[157] For 'that is the calling of Christians, that is our apostolic task, the desire which should consume our soul: to make this kingdom of Christ a reality, to eliminate hatred and cruelty, to spread throughout the

81

earth the strong and soothing balm of love' (Christ passing 183). 'We must work so that everyone with God's grace can live in a Christian way, "bearing one another's burdens" (Gal 6:2), keeping the commandment of love which is the bond of perfection and the essence of the law: cf Col 3:14 and Rom 13:10' (Christ passing 157).

'The understanding we must show is a proof of Christian charity on the part of a good child of God. Our Lord wants us to be present in all the honest pursuits of the earth, so that there we may sow, not weeds, but the good seed of brotherhood, of forgiveness, of charity and of peace. Never consider yourself anybody's enemy.

'A Christian has to be ready to share his life with everyone at all times, giving to everyone the chance to come nearer to Christ Jesus. He has to sacrifice his own desires willingly for the sake of others, without separating people into watertight compartments, without pigeon-holing them or putting tags on them as though they were merchandise or dried-up insects. A Christian cannot afford to separate himself from others because, if he did that, his life would be miserably selfish. He must become "all things to all men, in order to save all men" (1 Cor 9: 22).

'If only we lived like this, if only we knew how to saturate our behaviour with the good seed of generosity, with a desire for understanding and peace! We would encourage the rightful independence of all men. Each person would take on his own responsibility for the tasks that correspond to him in temporal matters. Each Christian would defend other people's freedom in the first place, so that he could defend his own as well. His charity would lead him to accept others as they are — because everyone, without any exception, has his weaknesses and makes his mistakes. He would help them, with God's grace and his own human refinement, to overcome evil, to remove the weeds, so that we can all help each other in living according to our dignity as human beings and as Christians.'[158]

And in this setting of friendship and understanding there will develop a spontaneous and natural apostolic conversation which will touch on the ultimate meaning of life; this will show us that 'we have been put here on earth for a further purpose: to enter into communion with God himself' (Christ passing 100); it will raise our minds up towards the fullness to which everything is destined, in such a way that peace and joy can be based on our sense of divine filiation and can impregnate our whole life: can fill even those things which seem capable of destroying peace and joy i.e. pain, suffering, death — those inseparable companions who have shared our way since sin first appeared on the scene.

'Christian optimism is not something sugary nor is it a human optimism that things will "work out well". No, its deep roots are awareness of freedom and faith in grace. It is an optimism which makes us be demanding with ourselves. It gets us to make a real effort to respond to God's call'.[159] It's a question of optimism which is aware of the real drama of history but which rises to it, lives it with faith. For, 'we have to fight vigorously to do good', but 'we should also be aware that even if we achieve a reasonable distribution of wealth and a harmonious organisation of society, there will still be the suffering of illness, of misunderstanding, of loneliness, of the death of loved ones, of the experience of our own limitations' (Christ passing 168). And there are no simplistic solutions: 'Faced with the weight of all this, a Christian can find only one genuine answer, a definitive answer: Christ on the cross, a God who suffers and dies, a God who gives us his heart opened by a lance for the love of us all' (Christ passing 168). 'Jesus on the cross, with his heart overflowing with love for men, is such an eloquent commentary on the value of people and things that words only get in the way. Men, their happiness and their life, are so important that the very Son of God gave himself to redeem and cleanse and raise them up' (Christ passing 165).

That is why the Christian, looking at Christ's cross, can recognise in suffering 'the touchstone of Love' (Way 439): it is a privileged opportunity to put faith into practice, to refine one's hope, to purify one's charity – in fact to unite oneself with Christ himself, to share in his redeeming death and, through it and in it, in his glorious resurrection, in the fullness of the Holy Spirit who fills the soul with a joy which nothing can destroy. Therefore, the 'supernatural acceptance of suffering was, precisely, the greatest of all conquests. By dying on the cross Jesus overcame death. God brings life from death. The attitude of a child of God is not one of resignation to a possibly tragic fate; it is the sense of achievement of someone who has a foretaste of victory. In the name of this victorious love of Christ, we Christians should go out into the world to be sowers of peace and joy through everything we say and do. We have to fight – a fight of peace – against evil, against injustice, against sin. Thus do we serve notice that the present condition of mankind is not definitive. Only the love of God, shown in the heart of Christ, will attain the glorious spiritual triumph of men' (Christ passing 168).

We can conclude our essay with some paragraphs which show the theological depth of Monsignor Escrivá de Balaguer's thought at its most expressive and which evidence conclusively his sense of divine 83 filiation and his invitation to 'sanctifying work, sanctifying yourself in work and sanctifying through work':

'In the life of Christ the resurrection and Pentecost were preceded by Calvary. This is the order that must be followed in the life of any Christian. . . . The Holy Spirit comes to us as a result of the cross — as a result of our total abandonment to the will of God, of seeking only his glory and renouncing ourselves completely.

'Only when a man is faithful to grace and decides to place the cross in the centre of his soul, denying himself for the love of God, detaching himself in a real way from all selfishness and false human security, only then — when a man lives by faith in a real way — will he receive the fullness of the great fire, the great light, the great comfort of the Holy Spirit.

'It is then, too, that the soul begins to experience the peace and freedom which Christ has won for us. . . . In the midst of the limitations that accompany our present life, in which sin is still present in us to some extent at least, we Christians perceive with a particular clearness all the wealth of our divine filiation, when we realize that we are fully free because we are doing our Father's work, when our joy becomes constant because no one can take our hope away.

'It is then that we can admire at the same time all the great and beautiful things of this earth, can appreciate the richness and goodness of creation, and can love with all the strength and purity for which the human heart was made. It is then that sorrow for sin does not degenerate into a bitter gesture of despair or pride, because sorrow and knowledge of human weakness lead us to identify ourselves again with Christ's work of redemption and feel more deeply our solidarity with other men. It is then, finally, that we Christians experience in our lives the sure strength of the Holy Spirit, in such a way that our failures do not drag us down. Rather they are an invitation to begin again, and to continue being faithful witnesses of Christ at all the crossroads of our life on earth.[160]

# IV EPILOGUE:

## TOWARDS A THEOLOGY OF WORK

In these pages I have outlined some of the main characteristics of Opus Dei. I should like to add a few final remarks by way of summary.

In my short survey of the history of spirituality I indicated the important position occuped by the spirit of Opus Dei – due precisely its being based on work, on an understanding of work which is quite unprecedented.[161] For, in the first place it views work not as a mere ascetical device, nor just as the setting in which a person lives – but as something which can be sanctified. It does not speak of a life of work and a life of holiness regarded as two different worlds, set on different planes, but of a genuine *'unity of life'*: it is through work itself, through the job which each person carries out, that he or she meets God.

There is a third element which shows up the deep implications of the other two, work and holiness: the spirit of Opus Dei speaks not just of work but of work in the world, carried out by people who are men and women of the world: everyday, professional, lay, secular work – each person doing a job for which he is known by the people around him, a job which defines his position in society and provides a framework for his whole life. This is the reason why the spirit of Opus Dei is something really new in the history of spirituality. Previously spirituality had paid attention to physical work done in the monastery, and to work in the sense of ecclesiastical work: but it had spoken hardly at all about work in the world, everyday work. Whereas the essence of the spirit of Opus Dei is that it proclaims that 'there is no noble human activity on earth that cannot be divinised, sanctified . . . . Work is intimately linked with the very essence of the spirituality proper to members of Opus Dei – work in the sense of practising one's own profession or trade, important or humble by human standards, though in God's eyes the standing of a job depends on the supernatural standing of the person doing it' (31 May 1954).

This then is the novelty of the spirit of Opus Dei and even now, fifty years after Opus Dei's foundation, there is still a newness to it. It does not propose any new ascetical techniques or new apostolic methods; rather, it projects a new, penetrating light onto the same old human experience – ordinary, everyday life and work. That is the charism – the gift of God – which makes Opus Dei what it is; and since 1928 this message has been making its way through the Church. In so doing it has done a great deal to give people a new awareness of certain truths of the Gospel – especially, the universal call to holiness, and with that the affirmation of the specific role of lay people and their position within the ecclesial community, with all that this implies: 'the legitimate personal freedom of people, the duty each has to bear the responsibility which corresponds to him in the field of earthly tasks; the obligation to defend also the freedom of others, as one's own, and to live in harmony with everyone; the charity of taking other people as they come – for each of us has faults and makes mistakes – , helping them with the grace of God and with human elegance to overcome these defects so that we may all help each other worthily to bear the name of Christian' (24 March 1931).

From the very beginning of his apostolate the founder of Opus Dei proclaimed that 'all the ways of the earth can be an opportunity for a meeting with Christ' (24 March 1930). 'Since the foundation of the Work in 1928', he said in an interview years later, 'my teaching has been that holiness is not reserved for a privileged few. All the ways of the earth, every state in life, every profession, every honest task can be divine' (Conversations 26). That is why Opus Dei is so important in the history of lay, secular spirituality; the specific spirituality of Opus Dei is not the only possible secular spirituality (in the sphere of supernatural life there is no room for monopolies) but it is also true that for over fifty years Opus Dei has represented something more than one spirituality among many, for it has played a major role in bringing about the new awareness of the spiritual characteristics proper to those Christians who live in and are part of the world, sanctifying that world, sanctifying themselves in it and sanctifying others through it.

At the start of this essay I suggested that the core of Opus Dei's contribution is Monsignor Escrivá's teaching on work and particularly his insistence on ordinary life as something which, with the help of grace, can be sanctified and can sanctify people. We have here two factors which are so closely linked that each has great influence on the other – the affirmation of the universal call to holiness, on the one hand, and the recognition of the Christian value of the world and of secular occupations on the other. Only if we look at things from a secular standpoint are we able to see work as something which makes people holy; and vice versa: only if we recognise the contribution that everyday work and ordinary life can make to Christian living, only then can we form a full picture of what being an ordinary Christian really means. It was the combination of these two factors that allowed spiritual theology to take that significant step forward which I have been referred to in my description of the spirituality of Opus Dei.

However, in these final remarks I want to go outside the scope of spiritual theology — to touch on the implications of this development for dogmatic theology too.

'Today we are far from having developed a "theology of work", to use a modern expression': since these words were written, in the early fifties, a certain progress has been made and many essays and monographs have appeared — some of them full of insight — but there is still a long way to go.

A theology of work involves analysing and evaluating work from the standpoint of the faith, with a view to determining work's place in human life and in the shaping of the cosmos, in the light of what Christian revelation has to say. This implies, in turn, a philosophical study of the phenomenon of work and an in-depth theological study of human existence as the setting of work. Looking at this from the historical point of view, we would first have to go to the Greeks: there we will find many valuable intuitions; and the same can be said of patristic and medieval Christian writers, not only because of their meditations on the nature of man and his purpose but also because of what they say on many questions directly connected with work. However, it is only from the Renaissance onwards and especially in the contemporary period that this subject really begins to be tackled.[162]

One factor which has helped stimulate this process of reflection — so some historians say — is the changes in the world of work which have taken place in the modern period as a result of scientific discovery and technological advances. The way was opened to tackle the philosophical study of work once we got over the kind of romanticism which idealised the farmer and the craftsman — and this happened when people realised work's huge capacity to transform the world around them, when they understood the implications which (also in the intellectual field) resulted from the changeover from tool to machine. Technology, it is said, given its ability to control and direct the energies of the universe means that man can feel he is not just an inhabitant of the world but also a builder of the world. All this has been an incentive to people to re-read the Christian message and take it in at a much deeper level.

Thus, the theology of work is a result, at least in part, of that phenomenon which the constitution *Gaudium et spes* refers to in general terms: 'The Church is not unaware how much it has profited from the history and development of mankind. It profits from the experience of past ages, from the progress of the sciences and from the riches hidden in various cultures, through which greater light is thrown on the nature of man and new avenues to truth are opened up'.[163]

I am sure there is something in all this, but I am not so sure which has caused which. I mean: is it the rise of technology which has lead to a change of attitude towards work, or it is the appearance of a new spiritual evaluation of work that has led to the development of technology? Whichever is the case from the strictly historical point of view, the important thing in developing a theology of work is to show the intimate connections between spirituality of work and theology of work and, in particular, the positive influence of the former on the latter.

Theological reflection and the strictly intellectual approach to what human work is and what it presupposes can be hindered by a certain 'spiritualism' and 'mysticism'. This is a very real danger because for long periods of time 'the ascetical aspect of work has clouded its human meaning';[164] indeed in certain sectors this still happens — which is why I have gone to some trouble to expose this mistaken approach. But the cause of it is not to be laid at the door of spirituality as such: it is caused by underdeveloped or deformed spirituality. It is important to stress this because otherwise we run an even greater risk — that of moving from an affirmation of secularity to the adoption of *secularist* stand: moving from a Christian to a naturalistic view of the world.

If we recall the quotations we have used from Monsignor Escrivá de Balaguer we will notice there is a change of accent between the earlier and later texts: this reflects the changes which were taking place in the environment in which they were written. In the early years the founder of Opus Dei found himself in an environment which identified holiness with withdrawal from the world, and apostolate with ecclesiastical involvements; consequently he had to proclaim boldly and defend vigorously the Christian value of human realities; he had to repeat again and again that secular occupations, earthly involvements — the world, in a word — did not constitute a profane universe which distracts man's attention and makes it difficult for him to reach God: no, the world is a proper place for man to meet Christ and bear witness through his deeds, to that meeting.

To some people what he said sounded like heresy; but he held his ground because he knew that his preaching was not the result of creative speculation; rather, he was translating into real life and into doctrine the express will of God which he came to know on 2 October 1928 and in the light of which he was able to understand the Gospel so much better.[165] The approval which the Holy See gave Opus Dei and the subsequent declarations of the Second Vatican Council on the universal call to holiness corroborated what the founder of Opus Dei had been saying and teaching. These later events, Monsignor Escrivá was to see, led to a whole series of approaches which indeed proclaimed the value of the world and of secular life – but from a non-theological perspective: this led to ambiguous positions being taken up in which the Christian dimension was *not* clearly affirmed: in fact there was the danger that it could be lost sight of. Hence his protest – reflected in the more recent texts quoted – and his continuing to plough his furrow: he was not engaging in a new intellectual and spiritual battle but rather continuing the old one. For – and this is the point I want to emphasise – if we recognise the truth of the Christian faith, one conclusion is inevitable: either we affirm the value of secular things from the standpoint of God or our affirmation of this value is inadequate.

In other words, a spirituality which takes in work in all its fulness is not an obstacle to a theology of work: rather, it is an impulse which creates that theology and ensures it goes in the right direction. Firstly, it is a creative contribution: because a spirituality which takes seriously the work done in the world, with all its anthropological and social implications, calls for a deep theological outlook which is not content with some more or less apt quotation from the Gospel but instead tries to reach the very nub of the question, showing forth the role of work in the building of the universe, analysing the exigencies of justice and harmonious social living which the Christian must confront, emphasising the position of work in a cohesive anthropology. And secondly, it sends the theology of work off in the right direction: because a genuine Christian life, a search for God, a search for him through work itself, anchors the heart in that supernatural core from which the intelligence also must start out.[166]

Without pretending to cover all the ground but just by way of example, I should like to suggest some of the lines I think need to be developed if we are aiming at a theology of work.[167]

(1) *Work and the building of the universe.* Man exists in the world; he forms part of a universe with which he is intimately united and whose destiny he is part of, even though he transcends it. The Genesis narrative[168] must be laid hold of and used as the starting point for the theological study of work. The view of the universe given us by Saint Thomas Aquinas is very helpful in this respect: what gives shape to the structure 89

of created things is precisely the inter connection of causalities; the unity of the universe is a unity of actions.[169] The modern transformation of work, as it moves from craftsman to technical personnel, helps to throw this aspect into relief: technology is defined precisely by a rationalisation of work methods which derives from discovering the laws of nature and aims at an even more developed organisation of human life.

But if these reflections help, as I said, to situate man in the universe, in themselves they are insufficient. They would do for an atheistic view of things which argues that the very meaning of history is to be found in this development of the universe; but they will not do for anyone, like the Christian, who knows that time will come to an absolute end due to God's free intervention in history. Besides, even an analysis of contemporary society leads one to recognise that the organisation of work and all that that involves (automation, concentration of power etc.) can lead to the alienation of the individual. The theology of work requires, therefore, that the ultimate end of human existence — that is, man's orientation to God — be borne clearly in mind; it is against this background that work itself must be seen, if we are to show the place it occupies in the unfolding of this ordination or calling.

(2) *Work and vocation.* The desire for the absolute which characterises the human person means that only in God does man find the full satisfaction of his yearnings. God's vigorous intervention in history shows man how great a gift his calling is — and, by contrast, the vacuous nature of any human project which is closed within itself. These central truths of the Christian faith must illuminate a theology of work: it will be a theology only to the extent that it shows the reference to God which work involves; from this we can see, for example, the radical insufficiency of any study of work which excludes the subject of prayer, of contemplative life, and, in broader terms, which does not include or fails to use as its starting point an awareness that man is a being open to God and is called to a living communion with him. And all that — in keeping with a truth I have pointed to often in the course of this essay — showing that the theological dimensions are not just juxtaposed to work but that both these dimensions and work itself are integrated in one and the same view of human existence. In each Christian life the various facets (the task the person has received, work, contemplative life, the part one plays in the ecclesial community, in civil life, etc.,) will have to be fused into a unity which signifies his full response to his vocation.

90    (3) *Work and eschatology.* If man is making his way towards his last

end by living his earthly existence to the full, we can ask a further question: at the end of time, what will remain of all the product of human endeavour?

Throughout the centuries, various thinkers with a monistic approach have argued that global history and earthly history are one and the same. In reply to them it has to be pointed out that the subject of history taken in its universality or fullness is not only mankind living on the earth, but the Mystical Body, the whole Church, which is both heavenly and earthly;[170] and the new heaven and the new earth of which the *Apocalypse* speaks are a free, supernatural gift, the result of God's lordly intervention bringing history to a close (cf Apoc 21: 1ff).

Other thinkers have offered dualistic solutions, maintaining that between the present character of the universe and the new world of eschatology there is no kind of connection or continuation. The world of history will be destroyed and the new heaven and new earth will arise as an effect of God's omnipotence — something quite unrelated to the history which has gone before. This approach aims at protecting the transcendence of God's free gift. However, this does not seem to be an adequate solution. For, recognising that the kingdom of heaven is essentially a free gift, and a gift which one reaches by means of grace, through death, what ought to be affirmed is that, at the end of time, what will be transformed will be not *any* world but *this* world, that is, the world which has been shaped by work and human effort. In other words, the new heaven and new earth are now being prepared by human work, although in an unclear and imperfect way. Thus Vatican Council II in *Gaudium et spes* 39, after stressing that 'earthly progress must be carefully distinguished from the growth of Christ's kingdom', states that 'after we have obeyed the Lord and in his Spirit nurtured on earth all the good fruits of nature and of our enterprise, we will find them again, but freed of stain, burnished and transfigured. This will be so when Christ hands over to the Father a kingdom eternal and universal; a kingdom of truth and life, of holiness and grace, of justice, love and peace'. Any attempt to deal with this question must occur within these two coordinates: although they don't provide a complete answer they do situate the right answer.

(4) *Work and suffering.* The penitential aspect of work has constantly been emphasised by spiritual authors, sometimes excessively. This one-sided approach must be corrected — without making the opposite mistake: the expiatory character of work or, better, of the effort which accompanies work, is something which must always be borne in mind; not only because in real life work involves tiredness and suffering  91

but because it brings into play fidelity to the Christian faith itself. Redemption implies the cross, and Christian optimism is not the kind that trusts in an inexorable progress of the universe: the optimistic Christian is he who, enlivened by Christ, battles against the forces of sin, in hope of victory. A study of work which forgot these features would not be fully Christian. Therefore, we ought to say, linking this aspect with the three previous ones, that suffering does accompany work – as it does all features of present human existence – but it does not in itself provide a definition of work: suffering is a feature of work's role in the economy of salvation, but it presupposes that work already forms part of that economy. Hence it should not be a starting-point for a theology of work: it is something to be brought into the picture once that theology is begun – in the same sort of way that the idea of Redemption is not located at the beginning of theology but is preceded by the ideas of creation and elevation to the supernatural level.

The lines I have just sketched are very schematic and general and should not be judged as if they were in any way well worked out. Let me round them off by some quotations from the Second Vatican Council texts: 'Throughout the course of the centuries, men have laboured to better the circumstances of their lives through a monumental amount of individual and collective effort. To believers, this point is settled: considered in itself, such human activity accords with God's will. For man, created to God's image, received a mandate to subject to himself the earth and all that it contains, and to govern the world with justice and holiness; a mandate to relate himself and the totality of things to him who was to be acknowledged as the Lord and Creator of all. Thus, by the subjection of all things to man, the name of God would be wonderful in all the earth. . . . Thus, far from thinking that works produced by man's own talent and energy are in opposition to God's power, and that the rational creature exists as a kind of rival to the Creator, Christians are convinced that the triumphs of the human race are a sign of God's greatness and the flowering of his own mysterious design.

'Christ's Church, trusting in the design of the Creator, acknowledges that human progress can serve man's true happiness. Yet she cannot help echoing the Apostle's warning: "Be not conformed to this world" (Rom 12:2). By the world is here meant that spirit of vanity and malice which transforms into an instrument of sin those human energies intended for the service of God and man. . . . All human activity, constantly imperilled by man's pride and deranged self-love, must be purified and perfected by the power of Christ's cross and resurrection.'

'We do not know the time for the consummation of the earth and of humanity. Nor do we know how all things will be transformed. As deformed by sin, the shape of this world will pass away. But we are taught that God is preparing a new dwelling place and a new earth where justice will abide, and whose blessedness will answer and surpass all the longings for peace which spring up in the human heart. Then, with death overcome, the sons of God will be raised up in Christ. What was sown in weakness and corruption will be clothed with incorruptibility. While charity and its fruits endure, all that creation which God made on man's account will be unchained from the bondage of vanity.'[171]

These paragraphs from *Gaudium et spes* provide, in summary form, most of the structural elements of the theology of work. To recognise them and develop them is one of the tasks which theology can and should continue to pursue. There is a great deal of work to be done — and, as I have stressed, it must be done from a truly theological perspective: to my mind, a full theology of work is really possible only if it is accompanied by a real awareness of man's divine vocation and of the value which work has in the dynamics of the spiritual life.

# NOTES

1. For the full text of this address cf., for example, *Studi Cattolici* 176 (Milan 1975), p. 612.

2. A. del Portillo, 'Mons. Escrivá de Balaguer, testigo de amor a la Iglesia' in *Palabra* 130 (Madrid 1976), pp. 205-210.

3. *L'Osservatore Romano*, 20/21 August 1979.

4. In *Il Gazzettino* (Venice), 25 July 1978.

5. In *Avvenire* (Milan), 26 July 1975.

6. Vatican Council II, Dogm. Const. *Lumen gentium* 31.

7. On this subject see Alvaro del Portillo, *Faithful and Laity in the Church* (Shannon 1972) which also includes quotations from Monsignor Escrivá on this subject.

8. *Lumen gentium* 40 and 41.

9. I develop this subject in 'La llamada universal a la santidad' in a collective work, *La vocación cristiano* (Madrid 1975), pp. 15-46.

10. *Populorum progressio* 27; see also 28 where he also recalls the ambivalent character which work shares with every temporal, intra-historical reality.

11. Cf. Saint Thomas, *Summa theologiae*, 1, q. 103, a.6.

12. *Apostolicam actuositatem* 4.

13. Address to the Association of Catholic Lawyers, 15 December 1963 in *Insegnamenti di Paolo VI*, I (Vatican City 1963), p. 609.

14. Jacques Maritain in *Le paysan de la Garonne* (Paris 1966), pp. 73-79, argues very strongly that spiritual theology has been affected by a type of disguised manicheism stemming from the disregard for the world one finds in the great mystics, especially Saint John of the Cross. This quasi-manicheism made it impossible to arrive at a positive appreciation of temporal realities, including that ordinary work which the Christian lay person carries out in the world, knowing that he is part of the world.

15. Cardinal G. Montini, 'Un grande problema del giorno: Religione e Lavoro' in *L'Osservatore Romano*, 1 April 1960.

16. Address to the ninth congress of ACLI (an Italian association of young workers) in *Insegnamenti di Paolo VI*, III (Vatican City 1965), pp. 16-17.

17. Paul VI, Address at the opening of the second session of Vatican Council II in *AAS* 54 (1963), p. 847.

18. *La Constitución apostólica 'Provida Mater Ecclesia' y el Opus Dei* (Madrid 1948), p. 7.

19. Michael Schmaus, *Katholische Dogmatik,* section 170, Munich 1959.

20. Cf. J. H. Newman, *Essay on the Development of Christian Doctrine*; throughout this work and especially at the beginning Newman shows that a religion really lived needs dogmatic development (London 1904) pp. 57-74. The first edition dates from 1845.

21. It is interesting to note, for example, that some of the Magisterium's statements on the role of work in the spiritual life arose in this context especially in connection with new liturgical feast days, such as that of the Holy Family (Leo XIII, 1892): *AAS* (ed. Victorio Piazzesi, 25, 1892), 8-10 or that of Saint Joseph the Worker (Pius XII, 1955): *AAS* 47, (1955), pp. 402-407; 48 (1956), pp. 226-237 and 287-292.

22. For example, to take a few: P. Dabin, *Le sacerdoce royale des fidèles*, 2 vols, (Paris 1945 and 1950); G. Thils, *Théologie des réalités terrestres* (Louvain 1946); Y.M. Congar, O.P., *Lay People in the Church*, first published in Paris in 1953 (chapter nine deals with sanctification in the world); various authors, *Cristo Lavoratore*, Rome 1955; M. D. Chenu, *The Theology of Work: an exploration* (Paris 1955), Dublin 1963); various authors, *Il lavoro nella vita spirituale*, Milan 1961. The very fact that most of the sources available are in article form (though some contain valuable insights) shows that the subject is only beginning to be explored.

23. Acknowledgement of this has become more widespread since Monsignor Escrivá's death: cf. for example articles by cardinals of the Catholic Church: Albino Luciani (later John Paul I) in *Il Gazzettino* (Venice) 25 July 1978; Sergio Pignedoli in *Il Veltro* (Rome 1975), n. 3-4; M. González Martin in *ABC* (Madrid), 24 August 1975; S. Baggio in *Avvenire* (Milan), 26 July 1975; J. Rosales in *Philippines Evening Express* (Manila), 26 June 1976; A. Rossi in *O Estado de S. Paolo* (Sao Paolo), 27 June 1976; F. Koenig in *Corriera della Sera* (Milan), 9 November 1975; J. Carberry in *The Priest* (Huntingdon, Ind.), June 1979; L. Aponte in *El Visitante de Puerto Rico*, 11 February 1979; P. Parente in *L'Osservatore Romano*, 24 June 1979.

24. I often speak in this essay of 'spirituality' and 'spiritualities'. I do not wish to try to specify the exact meaning of these words but I should like to stress the essential unity of Christian spirituality: there is no Christianity outside identification with Christ. The meaning I intend in each case is usually clear from the context. Cf. what I have written on this subject in *Gran Enciclopedia Rialp* vol. 9 (Madrid), pp. 206-209.

25. Reported in *L'Osservatore Romano*, 22/23 November 1965.

26. This interview was published in *Le Figaro* on 16 May 1966.

27. Regarding this date and Monsignor Escrivá's life in general cf. Alvaro del Portillo's essay in *En memoria de Mons. Josemaría Escrivá de Balaguer* (Pamplona 1976), pp.15-60 and Salvador Bernal: *Monsignor Josemaría Escrivá de Balaguer: A Profile of the Founder of Opus Dei* (Dublin 1977).

28. For commentaries on this text of Genesis, cf. *Conversations* 24 and *Friends of God* 57, 81 and 169.

29. For other commentaries on Jesus' work cf. *Conversations* 14 and 70; *Christ is passing by* 20 and 22; *Friends of God* 56, 81 and 121.

30. Cf. Jn 21:3 and commentary on same in *Friends of God* 264.

31. Cf. for example: Act 20:34; 1 Cor 4:12;2 Cor 11:12; 12:13; Eph 4:28; 1 Thes 4:11; 2 Thes 3:8-10.

32. *The Didache*, or *The Teaching of the Twelve Apostles* in *Ancient Christian Writers*, Vol. 6, trans. James A. Kleist, S.J., (Westminster 1948), p. 23. Cf. F.X. Funk, *Patres apostolici*, I, (Tubingen 1941), p. 30.

33. On work in Saint Benedict see Rembert Sorg, *Towards a Benedictine Theology of Manual Labor* (Lisle, Ill. 1951).

34. John Cassian, *De institutis coenobiorum*, Book II, 14, ed. M. Petschening in *Corpus scriptorum ecclesiasticorum latinorum*, XVII (Vienna 1888), p. 29.

35. St Athanasius, *Life of St Anthony*, 3 (MG 26, 844); see also St Benedict, *Regula Monasteriorum*, XLVIII, 8, in *Corpus scriptorum ecclesiasticorum latinorum*, LXXV, ed. R. Hanslik (Vienna 1950), p.116.

36. *De institutis coenobiorum* II, 12, ed. cit., pp. 28-29; cf. Saint Benedict, *Regula*, XLVIII, 1, ed. cit., p. 114.

37. Cassian tells this story at the end of his treatise on laziness: Book X, 24, *op. cit.*, pp. 192-193. For a more detailed study of work in monastic spirituality cf. *Yermo* 13

(Madrid 1975), pp. 3-352 and Pierre Minard, 'El trabajo en el monacato de vida simple' in *Yermo* 14 (Madrid 1976), pp. 161-175.

38. Cf. also *Conversations* 10.

39. Cf. A. del Portillo, essay in *En memoria . . .* op. cit., p. 48, and his 'Les professions . . .' in *La vie Spirituelle* 51 (Paris 1959), pp. 440-449 which deals with the concept of professional work.

40. Text dated 31 May 1954. It is not surprising that Monsignor Escrivá used the expression 'ordinary work' and 'professional work' as if they were inter-changeable, for the latter expression is always used in the sense of living in the world, sharing the common lot of ordinary people. He sees work as being a decisive element of living-in-the-world; other elements (marriage and involvement in politics, for example) are not essential to secularity: but work is. On this cf. J. Salinas 'Matrimonio, celibato y laicado' in *Palabra* 8 (Madrid 1966), pp. 7-10.

41. 'You are going to do apostolate from the most modest to the most important posts in society' (1 April 1934).

42. *Christ is passing by* 183. Cf. also *Conversations* 70.

43. On Monsignor Escrivá's contribution to these aspects of theology and spirituality cf. P. Rodriguez, 'La economía de la salvación y la secularidad cristiano' in *Scripta Theologica* 9 (Pamplona 1977), pp. 9-123.

44. It is significant that those Fathers who devoted more attention to the subject of work (Chrysostom, for example) were particularly concerned about the lives of ordinary Christians and tried to avoid identifying radical Christian life with monastic life because that would give the impression that the average Christian is not called to practice the Gospel teaching fully. Cf. for example, L. Daloz, *Le travail selon saint Jean Crysostome* (Paris 1939).

45. *Regula*, IV, 78, *op. cit.,* p. 35; cf. commentary on this in *San Benito, Su vida y su Regla* (Madrid 1956), p. 357.

46. Canons 2 and 3. Cf. Mansi, *Concilia*, XX, col. 933.

47. This called for taking a step which none of the earlier writers has intuited; its very size may explain why it was not taken. Cf., for example, the observations made by Congar on the monastic ideal as an expression of the substitution of the eschatological attitude found among the early Church by another, basically platonic, attitude based on a distinction between the perfect and the imperfect (or less perfect): Y. M. Congar, 'Vocabulaire et histoire de laicat', in *Les laics et la mission de l'Eglise* (various authors) (Paris 1962), pp. 13-17.

I think this judgment would be less harsh if we remembered that the great Fathers — and especially the Eastern Fathers — always tried to make clear the universal call to perfection and corrected the exaggerations of some writers. Cf. I. Hauser, 'Vocation chrétienne et vocation monastique selon les Pères', in *Laics et vie chrétienne parfaite* (various authors) (Rome 1963) pp. 33-116. Yet there is something in what Congar says. However, the key point lies not here but in the whole question of doctrinal developments — as we were discussing in the last section.

48. On magnificence and magnanimity cf. *Summa theologiae*, 2-2, qq. 129 and 134; on art 112, q. 27, a. 3. See also G. Cenacchi, *Il lavoro nel pensiero di Tommaso d'Aquino* (Rome 1977).

49. *Contra impugnantes Dei cultum et religionem*: especially chapters IV and VI (Whether religious are obliged to work with their hands; and Whether religious may live on alms). Cf. also *Quaestio disputata de caritate*, art. 19, where he describes secular occupations as an obstacle to contemplative life; he uses similar language in 2-2, q. 122 a.

4, ad 3. Again it might be noted that in *Tertia pars*, commenting on the life of Christ, he does not deal with his working years in Nazareth but goes directly from the presentation in the temple to the baptism of our Lord, considering all the intervening period under the heading of 'the entrance of Christ into the world' (q. 27, introduction); only then, i.e. in relation to the years of his public life, does he stop to consider Christ's life-style as if his early life had no importance. Similarly, when he asks why Christ postponed his baptism until he was thirty, he replies simply by explaining it in terms of the need for his reaching the mature and perfect age (q. 39, a.3).

50. Cf. Saint Bonaventure, *Quaestiones disputatae de perfectione evangelica*: art. 2 (on poverty in regard to begging; especially the answer to the ninth objection, and number 5 of the final answer); and art. 3 (on whether poor who are physically capable, and principally the Regulars, are universally obliged to manual work). It is interesting to note that his position is nuanced by the distinction he makes between manual work (that of farm labourers and artisans), civic work (that of rulers, military men and business people); and spiritual work, proper to those who are occupied in divine things. Significantly, the order followed by Saint Bonaventure is the inverse of that of St Thomas: first the lawfulness of begging and only then the obligation to work. However, the whole matter is left rather up in the air.

51. *Opere ascetiche di S. Bonaventura volgarizzate nel trecento*, cap. XV, 'Ora veggiamo come Jesù fece da dodici anni infino ai trenta anni' (Verona 1851), pp. 22-23. The *Meditationes vitae Christi*, one of the most widely-read spiritual books of the middle ages, was formerly attributed to Saint Bonaventure; modern scholarship indicates that it was in fact written by someone else, possibly the Franciscan Jacobo da Cordone: cf. C. Fisher, O.F.M., 'Die "Meditationes vitae Christi". Ihre handschriftliche Ueberlieferung und die Verfasserfrage', in *Archivum Franciscanum Historicum*, XXV (1923), pp. 3-35, 175-209, 305-348, 449-483.

52. On canonical aspects of it cf. S. de Angelis, *De fidelium associationibus*, I (Naples 1959), pp. 54-64; M. Durand, 'Confrérie' in *Dictionnaire de Droit Canonique*, IV (Paris 1935), col. 128-76.

53. *De Imitatione Christi*, Book 1, chap. 18. English version: trans. Knox and Oakley, London 1962, p. 43.

54. *De Imitatione Christi*, Book 1, chap. 22. Similar phrases in Book 1, chap. 25, 9; Book 3, chap. 26. The marked anti-intellectualism of the *Imitation*, together with the ascetical theory which these phrases reflect, may have influenced this attitude: cf., for example, Book 3, chap. 31.

55. Book 1, chap. 19; Book 3, chap. 39; Book 3, chap. 54; Book 1, chap. 25. The author of the *Imitation* likes to interpret in this way the words of Christ in Mt. 11:28; cf. Book 4, chap. 1.

56. It is difficult to find more pejorative remarks about work than those of Cisneros praising the excellence of the contemplative over the active life: according to him 'the contemplatives' dedicate themselves to that which pertains to the rational part of man; whereas the active 'eat and drink and make merry, they laugh and live lewdly and use their bodies, and in this way behave like beasts. Could such people possibly say that they help others with their works? Horses and donkeys do the same — and sometimes to more effect': *Ejercitatorio de la vida espiritual*, part 4, chap. 43, Madrid 1957, p. 217.

57. Cf. (a) for the use of the plural: *Ejercicios*, ninth annotation (ed. of the complete works of Saint Ignatius, edited by the Instituto Historico de la Compañía de Jesus en Roma, Madrid 1952, p. 155); idem, prayer on the first, second and third sin, 2nd point (*op. cit.*, p. 170); idem, prayer on the birth of Christ, 3rd point (*op. cit.*, p. 183); idem,

prayer on the life of Christ: from the last Supper to the Garden, 3rd note (*op. cit.,* 199); this meaning is very frequent in his letters (cf. *op. cit.,* index, pp. 1068-9).

(b) For the use of 'work' as equivalent to 'ascetical struggle': *Ejericios,* second week, prayer of the temporal king, 2nd part, first, second and third points (*op. cit.,* 179).

(c) I have not found 'work' used in the sense of human activity in the *Exercises;* on the other hand, it appears a few times in the *Constitutions* and the *Rules* of the Society to indicate a quality which the Superiors should have in their government or to refer to very confined aspects of the task of the novices (*Reglas del maestro de novicios,* 2nd part, no. 13; *op. cit.,* p. 614) or of the nurse (*Reglas del oficio de enfermero,* No. 3, *op. cit.,* p. 621. This also holds good for the use of 'work' by other Spanish spiritual writers of the period.

[The original of these texts is in Spanish (cf. *op. cit.,* pp. 140-142 and 356-357) and Fr Illanes has been dealing throughout with Spanish words 'trabajo' (work) and 'trabajos' (works) – Translator's note].

58. Cf. 'Censura del "Catecismo" de Carranza' in F. Caballero, *Conquenses ilustres,* II, *Vida del Ilmo. Sr. D. Fr. Melchor Cano* (Madrid 1871), p. 597.

59. Saint Thomas Aquinas, 2-2 q. 183; F. Suarez, *De virtute et statu religionis* (also called *De Religione*), tract. VII, Books I and VIII to X (in the *Opera omnia,* Paris 1856-1878). See also the classical exposition in Passerini, *De hominium statibus et officis* (Rome 1669) chap. 1 and J. Fornés, *La noción de 'status' en Derecho canónico* (Pamplona 1975).

60. *Introduction to the devout life,* trans. by John K. Ryan (London 1953) p. xxv. The book was first published in 1609. On the importance of Saint Francis de Sales in the history of spirituality see Paul VI, apostolic letter *Sabaudiae gemma* (29 January 1967) in *AAS* 59 (1967), 113-123.

61. It will be remembered that Saint Francis not only founded the Order of the Visitation but inspired many different religious societies and congregations; R. Perrin attempts to list these in *Dictionnaire de Theologie Catholique,* VI, col. 761.

62. Albino Luciani in *Il Gazzettino* (Venice), 25 July 1978.

63. This attitude was so deeply rooted that it is expressed even by authors whose zeal led them to engage in a very wide pastoral work among the laity. Take, for example, the case of Saint Alphonsus Mary Ligouri who wrote in his *Love of Our Lord Jesus Christ reduced to practice:* 'It is a great error to say God does not wish that we should all be saints: God desires, says Saint Paul (1 Thes 4:3), that we should be all saints, each in his own state, and according to his condition in life. The religious, the man in the world, the priest, the married man, the merchant, the soldier, all classes, in fine, ought to be saints, according to their state' (Chap. 8, pp. 72-73, in an undated English edition published by Duffy, Dublin). However, in his *Glories of Mary,* commenting on the presentation of the Virgin to the Temple he tells us that Mary 'knew that the world is full of dangers and that the sooner one leaves it, the sooner will he be free from its snares. And so this is what she sought to do at a very tender age. She shut herself up in the sacred retirement of the Temple...' (Part 2, Serm. 3, point 1, in the edition published in Dublin 1963, p. 36).

64. Although he did not deal with the matter at issue, since his work took place at the very beginning of contemporary period justice demands that I mention the admirable figure of Don Bosco who gave a great emphasis to work as a Christian means of sustaining and improving the social position of the needy, according to those words of Scripture, 'for the labourer deserves his food' (Mt 10:10).

65. *Epist. CXXV, ad Rusticum monachum,* no. 8 (PL 22,937).

66. Lecture given to religious men and women in Quebec in August 1963. Interestingly

enough, the Centro Studi della Unione Superiori Maggiori d'Italia included this lecture in *Rinnovamento e adattamento degli Instituti Religiosi* (Milan 1965), p. 59.

67. J. Herranz, 'The Evolution of the Secular Institutes' in *Irish Ecclesiastical Record*, October-November 1965, p. 272.

68. Vatican II's view of the religious state is based on these coordinates: '*By their state in life* (my italics) religious give splendid and striking testimony that the world cannot be transfigured and offered to God without the spirit of the beatitudes' (*Lumen gentium* 31); 'The People of God has no lasting city here below, but looks forward to one which is to come. This being so, the religious state by giving *its members greater freedom from earthly cares* more adequately manifests to all believers the presence of heavenly goods already possessed here below. Furthermore, it not only witnesses to the fact of a new and eternal life acquired by the redemption of Christ it foretells the resurrected state and the glory of the heavenly kingdom' (*Lumen gentium* 44). 'The members of each community should recall above everything else that by their profession of the evangelical counsels they have given answer to a divine call to live for God alone not only by dying to sin (cf. Rom 6:11) but also by renouncing the world (*Perfectae caritatis* 5).

69. Josemaría Escrivá de Balaguer, *La Constitución* . . . op. cit., p.20.

70. Ibid. p. 3.

71. The first edition of *The Way* entitled *Camino* dates from 1939 but the book grew out of a 1934 publication, *Consideraciones espirituales* which Monsignor Escrivá began to write in 1930 and part of which was published in multi-copy form in 1932. Where the text occurs in both books, in the Spanish original of the present book the author indicates also the *Consideraciones* source.

72. *Conversations* 24. Monsignor Escrivá referred to the early Christians as an example not only of work but of holy idealism (*Christ is passing by* 96), of apostolic enthusiasm (*Friends of God* 63 and 269), of prayer (*Christ is passing by* 134 and 153; *Friends of God* 242), of brotherhood (*Friends of God* 225), of sanctification of married life (*Conversations* 89; *Christ is passing by* 30); etc. On this aspect of Opus Dei's spirituality cf. R. Gomez Perez, *La fe y los dias* (Madrid 1973).

73. *La Constitución* . . . , op. cit., p. 19.

74. In speaking like this Monsignor Escrivá was fully aware of the spiritual and ecclesiological repercussions of what he was saying. That is why – on the same date in 1954 – he had no hesitation in saying that one of the obstacles to the development of a genuine lay and secular spirituality is the fact that 'some people are formed in an asceticism which is contrary to naturalness; with good intentions, of course, they cover their own personality or condition and put on a studied external appearance which does not suit them; people formed in this way cannot easily understand that what they see is really what is there, that the layman, for example, is a layman and not a religious posing as a layman; that the doctor is a doctor, the engineer an engineer, the teacher a teacher, the farmer a farmer, the mother a mother. They tend to see things and people as if they were acting out a comedy, wearing a mask, a costume which hides their real identity. It is good to remind these people that we – lay people or priests, all with a priestly soul and a lay outlook – have put into our life dedicated to the Lord's service, those words of Christ the Priest: "Sanctify them in the truth; thy word is truth" (Jn 17:17)'.

Indeed, the virtue of naturalness was always in the foreground of his preaching: cf. for example, *Friends of God* 90 and 192.

75. *Conversations* 66 and 62; cf. also 72. Cardinal Sergio Pignedoli has written on the same lines commenting on the spirit of Opus Dei: 'In the world the convinced Christian can have no inferiority complex nor should he pretend not to be what he is. He does not

need to "penetrate" the temporal sector – a phrase which is so often heard – since he is there already in his own right. The believer is not, nor can he be, even psychologically, a stranger to the world, because he, like anyone else, is a citizen in the full sense of the word'.

76. For more on this subject see what I have written in *Cristianismo, historia, mundo* (Pamplona 1973).

77. Cf. for example what Pedro Rodriguez has written in the essay 'La economía de la Salvación' quoted above.

78. R. Gomez Perez, 'Encontrarse siendo cristiano' in *Doctrina y vida* (various authors) (Madrid 1971), pp. 91ff.

79. Cf. what I have written under 'Vocación' in *Gran Enclicopedia Rialp*, vol. 23, pp. 658-662.

80. Cf. also 1 and 31-33.

81. Cf. Also *The Way* 832 and 837.

82. *The Way* 965. Both Saint Paul's text and Monsignor Escrivá's have to be read as theology, not as sociology. In other words, 'staying in the vocation in which God called you' is not intended to exclude changes which result from professional or social development etc. What is meant is that the Christian vocation does not, in itself, imply any change since it invites the person to sanctify the human situation in which he lives, whether this be stable or changing (depending on the circumstances of the person, etc., etc.). On this cf. P. Rodriquez, 'Sobre la espiritualidad de trabajo' in *Nuestro Tiempo* 35 (Pamplona 1971), p. 379.

83. *Conversations* 116. See also: *The Way* 776 (*Consideraciones espirituales*, p. 72) and 822; the long text quoted by P. Rodriquez in his essay 'La economía' referred to above, pp. 83-84; *Conversations* 88 and *Friends of God* 8 where he uses the comparison of Tartarín de Tarascón, who hunted for lions in the corridors of his house and, not finding them, was left empty-handed.

84. *The Way* 155; cf. *Christ is passing by* 58.

85. Decree *Primum Inter*, 16 June 1950: 'Omnes civiles honestas professiones maxima sollertia excercent: et quamvis profanae sint, socii, saepius renovata intentione, fervido interioris vitae cultu, continua atque hilari sui abnegatione, paenitentia duri tenacisque laboris qui sub omni respectu perfectus evadet, eas santificare iugiter satagunt'.

86. Cf. Saint Leo the Great, *Sermo de Nativitate Christi*, XXI, 3 (PL 54, 192).

87. *Christ is passing by* 134; cf. *Friends of God* 2-3 (a 1960 homily).

88. Cf. *Friends of God* 60 and *Christ is passing by* 46.

89. Cf. *Christ is passing by* 47; *Conversations* 60.

90. *Conversations* 114 and 116. Cardinal Franz Koenig, among others, has pointed to the importance of this homily: cf. *Corriere della Sera* (Milan), 26 July 1975.

91. *Conversations* 70. Cf. also what Monsignor Escrivá said (31 May 1954): 'Because we are not religious, as I have told you a thousand times since the foundation [of the Work] I am not interested in vows. What Opus Dei asks for is virtues, and it's by virtues that we will gain heaven. All we ask for is the practice of the human virtues and the supernatural virtues, which are the way to attaining Christian perfection – each person in his own state in life in the world – and so equip ourselves to serve all souls more effectively.

92. The spirituality of Opus Dei is radically christological and therefore sacramental: everything it affirms regarding Christian living presupposes the affirmation of the grace of baptism – enriched by the other sacraments, especially the Eucharist. On this P. Rodriquez 'Camino y la espiritualidad del Opus Dei' in *Teologia espiritual* 9 (Pamplona 1965), pp. 230-231.

93. For a fuller account of this see what I have written under the heading 'Mundo' in *Gran Enclicopedia Rialp*, vol. 16, pp. 450-451 and R. García de Haro, *'Homilías : Es Cristo que pasa'* in *Scripta theologica* 5 (Pamplona 1973), p. 397.

94. Decree *Primum inter*, 16 June 1950: ' . . . nascitur necessitas et veluti instinctus supernaturalis omnia purificandi, elevandi ad ordinem gratiae, sanctificandi et convertendi in instrumentum apostolatus'.

95. Text dated 31 May 1954. See also *Christ is passing by* 46; *Friends of God* 9; *Conversations* 70.

Cardinal Karol Wojtyla, now John Paul II, referred to this saying of the founder of Opus Dei in a lecture he gave in 1974 on the subject of 'Evangelisation and the inner man'. After emphasising that man's growth has to do with inner growth, he asks how does human development relate to technical progress and its consequences: 'How can man, in his effort to impose himself on the face of the earth, put his spiritual stamp on the world? . . . We can reply with a happy expression – which everyone knows so well – which Monsignor Escrivá de Balaguer has been using for so many years: 'by each person sanctifying his own work, sanctifying himself in his work and sanctifying others through his work'. This lecture is published in *La fe de la iglesia: textos del Card. Karol Woytyla* (Pamplona 1979), pp. 94-95.

96. See also *Christ is passing by* 23: where we find the same sort of statements as quoted in the previous note, but couched in terms of family life, in connection with marriage as a Christian vocation.

97. As Monsignor Escrivá put it in a text dated 31 May 1954: 'Everyday work . . . is not simply the environment in which the members of Opus Dei should seek Christian perfection: it is the means and the way that they use to attain it'.

98. *The Way* 334; see also *The Way* 332 and 336.

99. *Conversations* 10; see also 70.

100. Monsignor Escrivá put it graphically in this way (15 October 1948): 'We have a chronic illness in Opus Dei – work: a contagious, incurable and progressive illness; we don't know how to do nothing'. Cf. also *The Way* 356 and 358.

101. *Friends of God* 55; see also 58 and 62.

102. 'Through the exercise of one's own professional work in the middle of the world we seek also the temporal good of all mankind' (14 February 1950).

103. Already in *The Way* we read: 'Selfish. Always looking after yourself. You seem incapable of feeling the fraternity of Christ. In those around you, you do not see brothers: you see stepping stones (31; see also 32). This relationship between work and service is also developed by Monsignor Escrivá when he speaks of work promoting the growth of culture. Cf., for example, *The Way* 345 and the interview in *Conversations* 73ff and addresses in connection with the University of Navarre, especially those published in *Redacción* (Pamplona), November 1976. Cf. also F. Ponz Piedrafita's essay in *En memoria* . . . (Pamplona 1976), pp. 61-132.

104. *La Constitución. . . . ,* op. cit., p. 20.

105. For 'political activity, in the noble meaning of that expression, is nothing other than an act of service aimed in search of the common good of the earthly City' (9 January 1932).

106. *Christ is passing by* 182. Regarding this aspect of Monsignor Escrivá's spirituality cf. A. del Portillo, *On Priesthood* (Dublin 1980), pp. 11ff and J. Urteaga, *Man the Saint* (Dublin 1959).

107. We can find this attitude even in the early fifties in an essay by a Spanish theologian criticising certain texts on lay spirituality: 'Life in the world has always been hard and

restless and it becomes more so due to the fact that all the advances of civilisation create new needs. From the point of view of spirituality, these concerns may be a necessity but they are also a veritable temptation and a danger'. Basilio de S. Pablo, 'La perfección cristiana en el Laicado' in *XIII Semana Española de Teologia* (Madrid 1954), pp. 297-298.

108. On this see J. G. Torello's vigorous article on 'The Spirituality of Lay People' in *The Furrow* (Maynooth) April 1966, pp. 222-235 and his chapter on 'Condizione laicale' in *Tentazioni del laicato* (Milan 1966), pp. 5-38.

109. Key texts include *Lumen gentium* 34, 39, 41; *Apostolicam actuositatem* 4; *Presbyterorum ordinis* 14. I should like at this point to mention one small but interesting fact. On 25 November 1961 the Sacred Penitentiary issued a decree granting indulgences to those offering their work to God. The theological background to this decision is connected with our present subject – the relation between human tasks and supernatural calling. But almost twenty years before the Holy See issued this decree referring to all Christians it had issued a similar one referring to Opus Dei. In the Briefs *Cum Societatis* (28 June 1946) and *Mirifice de Ecclesia* (20 June 1947) Pius XII granted members of Opus Dei indulgences for aspirations they might say in the course of their work, manual or intellectual.

The *Enchiridium indulgentiarum* promulgated on 29 June 1968 follows the line of the 1961 decree by granting a partial indulgence to those who, in the course of their work and in general when confronting difficulties, raise their heart trustingly to God, adding even if only mentally a pious ejaculation.

110. 'Prayer', Monsignor Escrivá said in a homily in 1951, 'becomes continuous, like the beating of our heart, like our pulse. Without this presence of God, there is no contemplative life, our working for Christ is worth very little, for vain is the builder's toil if the house is not of the Lord's building': cf. Ps 126:1 (*Christ is passing by* 8).

111. Monsignor Escrivá's contribution to liturgical renewal has been discussed by Cardinal G. Lercaro in *Corriere della sera* (Milan) 25 June 1976; see also A. Livi, 'L'Opus Dei e il innovamento liturgico' in *Uno stile cristiano di vita* (various authors) (Milan 1972), pp. 78-95.

112. The very structure of *Consideraciones espirituales* and *The Way* imply this 'plan of life': it is synthesised in *Christ is passing by* 119 and *Friends of God* 149-152 and 248-249.

113. On this subject see the important homily 'Towards holiness' in *Friends of God* 294-316.

114. For a fairly complete historical account of all this see under 'Contemplation' in *Dictionnaire de Spiritualité* vol. II, col. 1643-2193.

115. This is in fact what happened in his own case. Cf., for example, what Bishop F. Hengsbach wrote in *Ruhrwort* (Essen), 23 August 1975): 'He lived and thought on completely supernatural lines. The reality of God, the presence of Christ in the most Blessed Sacrament of the altar, the reality of heaven, the saints (especially the Mother of God and Saint Joseph) – i.e. the real supernatural world – were for him *evident* facts'. And in *La Vanguardia* (Barcelona), 6 July 1975 a Spanish journalist, Manuel Aznar wrote: 'I can't remember anyone who so spontaneously, so naturally, united in one single whole the natural and the supernatural, God and man, man and God. The very difficult enterprise of keeping a hold on supernatural aspirations in the middle of the ordinary trivialities of human existence was achieved by the founder of Opus Dei with apparently no effort at all, not grumbling when it came to combining supernatural yearnings with the hard facts of everyday life'.

116. 'In our work, done facing God – in his presence – , let us pray without ceasing,

for when we work as our spirit asks us to we put into practice the theological virtues which crown Christian living. We practise faith, though our contemplative life, in this constant conversation with the Trinity present in our soul. We practise hope when we persevere in our work "knowing that, in the Lord, you cannot be labouring in vain" (1 Cor 15:58). We live charity, trying to put love of God into all our actions, spending ourselves in generous service to our fellow men, to all souls' (15 October 1948).

117. 'As I look up from the microscope, my sight comes to rest on the cross – black and empty. That cross without its Crucified is a symbol. It has a meaning which others cannot see. And though I am tired out and on the point of abandoning the job, I once again bring my eyes to the lens and continue: for the lonely Cross is calling for a pair of shoulders to bear it' (Way 277; see also 178).

118. A. del Portillo in his introduction to *Christ is passing by*, p.13.

119. 'What a wonderful thing it is to be a child! When a man asks a favour, his request must be backed by a list of his qualifications. When it is a child who asks – since children haven't any qualifications – it's enough for him to say: I'm a son of So-and-so. Ah, Lord, – say it to him with all your heart! – I am a son of God!' (*The Way* 892).

'We are children of God and we can talk things over with him and spend time with him, just as trustingly as a son does with his father' (*Friends of God* 145).

'How do you explain this confident prayer – this knowledge that we shall not perish in the battle? It is a conviction rooted in something which is always a cause of wonder to me: our divine filiation' (*Christ is passing by* 64).

120. 'If only we could live with more trust in divine Providence, strong in faith, in the certainty of God's daily protection which never fails, how many worries and anxieties we would be spared! Now that I am confiding in you as a friend, as a priest and as a father, I would like to remind you that in every circumstance of our lives we are, by God's mercy, children of our almighty Father, who is in heaven but who also dwells in the intimacy of our hearts' (*Friends of God* 116).

'Through the gift of piety, the Holy Spirit helps us to realise with certainty that we are children of God. And, being children of God, how can we be sad? Sadness is the end product of selfishness. If we truly want to live for God, we will never lack cheerfulness' (*Friends of God* 92).

'Can there be any joy to compare with that of the person who, knowing himself to be poor and weak, knows also that he is a son of God? . . . As I never tire of repeating: let them be sad who are determined not to recognise that they are children of God!' (*Friends of God* 108).

'"Father", said that big fellow, a good student at the university (I wonder what has become of him), "I was thinking of what you told me – that I'm a son of God! – and I found myself walking along the street, head up, chin out, and a proud feeling inside . . . a son of God!"

'With sure conscience I advised him to encourage that "pride"' (*The Way* 274).

121. 'There is only one race in the world: the race of the children of God. We should all speak the same language, taught us by our Father in heaven – the language Jesus spoke with his Father. It is the language of heart and mind, which you are using now, in your prayer – the language of contemplation, used by men who are spiritual, because they realise they are children of God. This language is expressed in a thousand motions of our will, in the clear insights of our minds, in the affections of our heart, in our commitment to lead a virtuous life, in goodness, happiness and peace' (*Christ is passing by* 13). See also *Christ is passing by* 106 and *Friends of God* 233.

122. Cf. P. Rodriguez, 'La economía . . . ', op. cit., p. 55ff.

123. I cannot here cover all Monsignor Escrivá's teaching on prayer; all I can do is touch on those points which help us understand the scope of what he has to say about sanctification of work and in work. I would like to point out, though, that he presents this warm, familiar sense of divine friendship as the result and the goal of a life of prayer centred on friendship with Christ, God and man, and particularly on Christ's humanity, grasped through contemplation of his whole life on earth – not just its high points (his death and resurrection) but also the ordinary situations of his simple life at Nazareth, which constituted a very special sign of God's closeness to our everyday lives. That is why he gave great importance to prayer to Mary and Joseph, who had Jesus so close and who therefore can lead us to him, help us to feel near him and to discover in his humanity his. divinity, in this way going from the 'trinity on earth' (Joseph, Mary, Jesus) to the 'trinity in heaven'. One of the most vivid indications of his prayer in this direction is his book *Holy Rosary* which dates from 1934 (latest English edition Dublin 1979). See also the homily 'Towards Holiness' in *Friends of God* 294-316.

124. On the virtue of magnanimity, so intimately connected with this point, see *Friends of God* 80 and 106.

125. *The Way* 813-830. See also *Conversations* 116; *Christ is passing by* 44, 77 and 148; and *Friends of God* 7-8, 41, 62, 221.

126. Connected with this is another important aspect of Monsignor Escrivá's spiritual doctrine, the life of childhood. See the two chapters in *The Way* (852-901) on this: they indicate the full reach of awareness of being children of God. See also *Christ is passing by* 64-66 and *Friends of God* 142-148 and the subject indexes to these two books.

127. *The Way* 813; see also *The Way* 418 and 429.

128. *Christ is passing by* 174; see also *Conversations* 18. Monsignor Escrivá often spoke along these lines during the catechetical journeys he made to different countries or to visitors he received in Rome; all these meetings put him into contact with people of the most varied work backgrounds and gave him an opportunity to show his appreciation for all of them. I would just give two examples, both from a visit he made to the University of Navarre in 1964. He received a group of university cleaners; among the things he said to them was: 'I do not know which is more important in the university, your work or that of the governing body'. During the same visit he met a group of miners: 'All types of work are equal before God: there are no positions of greater or lesser importance: the importance depends on the love of God put into the work by those who do it. Tell your companions for me that when they are working in the bowels of the earth they are not way down: they are very high up, for work dignifies them and brings them closer to God' *Telva* (Madrid), 15 December 1964.

129. Cf. *Christ is passing by* 106 and 122.

130. *Christ is passing by* 120; see also 106.

131. *Friends of God* 265, where he is commenting on Luke 5: 1ff. The doctrine on apostolate outlined in these two texts has many important implications for ecclesiology; but I cannot go into this matter here. Look, however, at this text (12 December 1952): 'Freedom – within due limits – and the responsibility that goes with it are the hallmark of lay activity: in apostolate as in everything else. Therefore, when professional, secular work is turned into an instrument of zeal for souls (personal witness to Jesus Christ in the middle of the world) a quiet work of apostolate is done in a way which statistics can hardly measure, since only our Lord can assess its effectiveness. It is an activity perfectly compatible with that done by members of ordinary official associations, and (although the manner of doing it is very different) it is always done with the obedience due to ecclesiastical authority; but *de iure* it is not a hierarchical task; it is not an ecclesiastical

apostolate, finding its concrete expression in the carrying out of a mandate or of a canonical mission. It is not a prolongation or *longa manus* of the hierarchy, but an earthly and divine task as well as an ecclesial one, truly appropriate to lay people; and in this way a deeper apostolate is done at all social levels because in this quiet and fruitful activity there always shines obedience to the Roman Pontiff and the bishops in communion with the Holy See, although it is done on the exclusive responsibility — I repeat — of a man who practises it with full freedom'. See also *Conversations* 9, 20-21, 58-59, 112. On this subject and especially on the important distinction (consecrated by the Vatican II texts) between the mission of the Church and the mission of the hierarchy (a very important one but it does not exhaust the former) see A. del Portillo, *Faithful and Laity in the Church* (Shannon 1972), pp. 41ff.

132. Decree *Apostolicam actuositatem* 2.

133. On lay apostolate carried out in a specific sphere — that of the family — see *Christ is passing by* 27ff and *Conversations* 89, 91, 92 and 96.

134. Decree *Primum inter*, 16 June 1950: 'Omnes et singuli [sodales Operis Dei] exemplo, quo semper et ubique inter cives, inter collegas, inter laboris socios, domi, in via, in officio optimos sese exhibere conantur . . . , Ecclesiae regnique caelestis actuosi ac indefessi operarii sunt'.

135. *Christ is passing by* 105. Monsignor Escrivá often quotes Saint Paul's text about the Christian having the *bonus odor Christi*: cf. *The Way* 842; *Christ is passing by* 36 and 156; *Friends of God* 271.

136. *The Way* 372. The previous point expresses the same idea in another way: 'When you see people of uncertain professional standing acting as leaders at public functions of a religious nature, don't you feel the urge to whisper in their ears: Please, would you mind being just a little less Catholic?' (*The Way* 371).

137. P. Rodriguez, 'la economía . . . ,' op. cit., p. 109.

138. *Conversations* 62. Other references to 'beginning to do and to teach' occur in *The Way* 342; *Christ is passing by* 21 and 182; *Friends of God* 115 and 163.

139. Cf. *Friends of God* 257-258.

140. Cf. *The Way* 1.

141. Cf. *The Way* 831.

142. Cf. *Apostolicam actuositatem* 2.

143. *Gaudium et spes* 38-39.

144. *Christ is passing by* 183. For other commentaries on this text of Saint John see *Christ is passing by* 14, 38, 105 and 156 and *Friends of God* 58.

145. *Christ is passing by* 99; see also homilies on 'The Supernatural Aim of the Church' and 'Loyalty to the Church' published by Scepter Press, New York, 1977.

146. *Christ is passing by* 124. See also 99.

147. Cf. *Friends of God* 93, 228.

148. Also: 'I do not see the commitment of Christians in the world as the springing up of a political-religious movement. That would be madness, even if it were motivated by a desire to spread the spirit of Christ in all the activities of men. What we have to do is put God in the heart of every single person, no matter who he is' (*Christ is passing by* 183). On this point see A. García Suarez, 'Existencia secular cristiano', *Scripta theologica* 2 (1970), pp. 155-159.

149. Therefore Monsignor Escrivá, although he knew and sometimes used the expression '*consecratio mundi*', preferred to speak of 'sanctifying from within'. See for example *Christ is passing by* 125 and *Conversations* 9 and 60.

150. For example: 'The spirit of Opus Dei, which I have tried to practise and to teach

for more than thirty-five years now, has made me understand and love personal freedom' (*Christ is passing by* 17). 'Throughout my years as a priest I should say that I have not so much spoken as shouted about my love for personal freedom' (*Friends of God* 32). 'I will keep on repeating that our Lord has gratuitously given us a great supernatural gift, divine grace, and another wonderful human gift, personal freedom' (*Christ is passing by* 184).

151. 'Las riquezas de la fe', in *ABC* (Madrid), 2 November 1969.

152. *Friends of God* 23; the quotation from Saint Augustine comes from Sermo 169, 13 (PL 38, 923).

153. This is the whole theme of the homily 'Freedom, a gift from God' in *Friends of God* 23-28; see also *Christ is passing by* 113, 129.

154. 'Las riquezas de la fe' in *ABC* (Madrid), 2 November 1969

155. Ibid. Many years earlier he had said: 'Avoid that abuse so common nowadays (it is easy to find, all over the world) which arises from a disregard for the lawful freedom of men: it tries to oblige everyone to form one single group in matters of opinion, seeking to create temporal dogmas, as it were; and to defend that mistaken approach by scandalous attacks on those who have the nobility not to give in to it' (9 January 1932).

156. The founder of Opus Dei spoke very often about freedom in temporal affairs – both in general and also with reference to members of Opus Dei who are ordinary citizens like everyone else since their involvement with Opus Dei in no way takes from their autonomy in social, political, cultural action. 'You enjoy full freedom and are personally responsible for your actions – not only doing your professional work but also in your social, cultural or political activity, things you have in common with the other citizens of your country. Each of you always acts with complete freedom, following his conscience' (9 January 1935). 'The Directors of the Work never impose a particular opinion in those areas which God has left to the free discussion of men. If at any time it be necessary for the good of souls to lay down a specific norm in these matters it is for the local ordinary and him only to give criterion, as part of his pastoral ministry' (2 October 1958).

The refinement with which he practised and saw to it that others practised this central aspect of the spirit and lifestyle of Opus Dei caused him to lay down that the Directors of the Work not only must not give any specific opinion on temporal matters but also, in their apostolic action, should avoid doing anything which could influence the opinions of those who came close to the Work: 'Do not talk politics, in the ordinary sense of the word, and avoid other people talking party or group politics in our houses. Make them see that all opinions which respect the rights of the Church fit in the Work' (9 January 1935).

This does not mean that the members of the Association may not act in the various areas of public life. The Holy See, in the decree of approval given to Opus Dei on 16 June 1950, affirms that the members should exercise all their rights and duties as citizens, 'nullo imprudenter excepto', and Monsignor Escrivá commented: 'Each member of Opus Dei, involving himself as much as he likes in politics, does so with the greatest freedom and therefore on his own responsibility, following his conscience as a citizen, without implicating other people in the decisions which he has legitimately taken' (7 October 1950).

See also *Friends of God* 11 and 170; *Conversations* 27-30, 38-39, 48-50, 64-65, 98, 117-119; and an interview in *ABC* (Madrid), 24 March 1971. On some of the ecclesiological implications of all this see also *Conversations* 5, 9, 11-12 and 58-59.

In this connection cf. for example: J. Herranz, 'El Opus Dei y la política' in *Nuestro Tiempo* 6 (Pamplona 1957), pp. 385-402, and 'Natura dell'Opus Dei e attività temporali dei suoi membri' in *Studi Cattolici* 31 (Milan 1962), pp. 73-90; Wilhelm Blank and Otto

B. Roegele's contributions in *Opus Dei, für und wider* (Osnabrück (1967), pp. 45-64 and 170-177; J.J. Thierry *L'Opus Dei, Mythe et realité* (Paris 1973), pp. 103-118; L.I. Seco, *La herencia de Mons. Escrivá de Balaguer* (Madrid 1976), pp. 57-64. On historical aspects related to Spain cf. my 'L'azione politica dei cattolici nella spagna d'oggi' in *Studi cattolici* 17 (Milan 1960), pp. 48-56 and R. Gomez Pérez, *Política y religión en el régimen de Franco* (Barcelona 1976), pp. 250-267.

157. *Christ is passing by* 168; see also *Friends of God* 105.

158. *Christ is passing by* 124. This text is a commentary on the parable of the wheat and the cockle; together with Saint Paul's *'Vince in bono malum'* (Rom 12:21), it is often used by the founder of Opus Dei and is the inspiration of one of his basic maxims: 'Drown evil in an abundance of good'. The fact of evil should not demoralise the Christian or cause him to retreat into a shell or become a bitter, violent zealot: it should urge him to grow in faith, in hope and in charity and to work consistently with that, realising that the good which he can produce contributes, with God's grace, to overcoming, to drowning evil.

159. *Christ is passing by* 114; see also 177.

160. *Christ is passing by* 137-138; see also *Friends of God* 132 and 141.

161. Cf., for example, what cardinals Luciani, Baggio, Koenig, etc., have written: note 23 above.

162. For a list of theological literature on work and allied subjects to 1964 cf. K. V. Truhlar, *Il lavoro cristiano* (Rome 1966), pp. 233-237. Subsequently work has been widely discussed due to the attention given to the problems of secularisation, economic and social liberation and marxist analyses of work: but all very partial studies.

163. *Gaudium et spes* 44.

164. Henri Sanson, *Spiritualité de la vie active* (Le Puy 1957), p. 212; cf. also pp. 9-11.

165. Cf. note 27 above.

166. Paul VI said that 'there is no time for humanism that does not tend towards the Absolute (*Populorum progressio* 42: 26 March 1967: AAS 59, 1967, 278) and John Paul II: 'the basic statement of this [Christian] anthropology is that man is the image of God' (address to the opening of the third general conference of Latin American bishops, Puebla, 28 January 1979). And of course all this holds good for a humanism based on work.

167. Cf. the heading 'Trabajo humano' in *Gran Enclicopedi*ǎ *Rialp*, vol. 22, pp. 657ff.

168. The Creation texts, especially Gen 2:15: 'Yahweh took the man and put him in the garden of Eden *to dress it*'.

169. Cf., e.g., *Summa theologiae*, I, q. 104, a. 2, ad. 1.

170. Cf. *Lumen gentium* 48-50.

171. *Gaudium et spes* 34, 37 and 39.